Death

This book examines how legal institutions reify the value of death in the twenty-first century.

Its starting point is that biotechnological innovations have extended life to such an extent that death has become an epistemological problem for legal institutions. It explores how legal definitions of death are subject to the governing logic of economisation, how legal technologies for registering a death reshape what kinds of deaths are counted during a pandemic, and how technologies for recycling cadaveric tissue problematise the legal status of the corpse. The question that unites each chapter is how legal institutions respond to technologies that bring death before their laws. The book argues for an interdisciplinary approach, informed by the writings of Georges Bataille, Wendy Brown, Georges Canguilhem, and Michel Foucault, to understand how legal epistemologies are increasingly disrupted, challenged, and countered by technologies that repurpose death to extend, nourish, and foster human life. It contends that legal theorists and social scientists need to rethink doctrinal perspectives of law when theorising how law defines the moment of death, shapes what kind of deaths count, and recycles the debris of the dead.

This book will appeal to a broad international readership with research interests in critical theory, political theory, legal theory, or death studies; and it will be particularly useful for teachers and students who are searching for an accessible entry point to the study of the intersections between law and death.

Marc Trabsky is an Associate Professor in Law at La Trobe University, Australia.

Part of the New Trajectories in Law
series
series editors
Adam Gearey, *Birkbeck College, University of London*
Prabha Kotiswaran, *Kings College London*
Colin Perrin, *Commissioning Editor, Routledge*
Mariana Valverde, *University of Toronto*

for information about the series and details of previous and forthcoming titles, see www.routledge.com/New-Trajectories-in-Law/book-series/NTL

A GlassHouse Book

Death

New Trajectories in Law

Marc Trabsky

Routledge
Taylor & Francis Group
a GlassHouse Book

First published 2024
by Routledge
4 Park Square, Milton Park, Abingdon, Oxon OX14 4RN

and by Routledge
605 Third Avenue, New York, NY 10158

*Routledge is an imprint of the Taylor & Francis Group,
an informa business*

a GlassHouse book

© 2024 Marc Trabsky

British Library Cataloguing-in-Publication Data
A catalogue record for this book is available from
the British Library

ISBN: 978-1-032-11922-9 (hbk)
ISBN: 978-1-032-11923-6 (pbk)
ISBN: 978-1-003-22216-3 (ebk)

DOI: 10.4324/9781003222163

Typeset in Sabon
by Apex CoVantage, LLC

This book is dedicated to the memory of Gérard
Hervé Emmanuel Flore

Contents

Acknowledgements

Research for this book was partly funded by an Australian Research Council Grant on 'Socio-Legal Implications of Virtual Autopsies in Coronial Investigations' (DE220100064). I would like to thank my colleagues at La Trobe University for providing a robust intellectual community and especially Averyl Gaylor for her excellent research assistance. I have benefited from workshopping early versions of chapters at several symposiums since 2019. I thank David Carter and Daniel Fleming for inviting me to think about the economisation of death during a workshop held at the University of Technology Sydney in 2019; Carl Stychin for organising a workshop on *Law and Humanities in a Pandemic* at the Institute of Advanced Legal Studies, University of London in 2020; and Rick Mohr, Patrícia Branco, and Francesco Contini for inviting me to talk about the normal and pathological during workshops held in 2020 and 2021.

I commenced this book a couple of months prior to the emergence of a global pandemic, and during the process of writing I witnessed the tragic deaths of Hervé Flore, and Courtney Hempton. These deaths haunted the completion of this book. In a way, the book became an attempt to make sense of these sudden deaths, or rather to remind myself that they will not be forgotten under the auspices of a pandemic. The idea for Chapter 2 arose from conversations that I had with Courtney during stringent public health restrictions in the second half of 2020, and I wish she were alive today so that we could continue that discourse.

I would like to thank Colin Perrin and Naomi Round Cahalin from Routledge, and the series editors of *New Trajectories in Law*, for their patience, encouragement, and support during the publication process. I am also grateful for the care provided by my friends and family. This book is indebted to Jacinthe Flore, not only for her close reading and insightful comments on the manuscript, but because she has changed the way that I think about death. Jacinthe is my most critical, considerate, and thoughtful interlocutor, and I am immensely thankful for her companionship.

Early versions of parts of this book have been published elsewhere, and I am appreciative for the permission to include a portion of those publications here: Marc Trabsky, 'Normalising Death in the Time of a Pandemic' (2022) 12(3) *Onati Socio-Legal Series* 540 <https://doi.org/10.35295/osls.iisl/0000-0000-0000-1232>; and Marc Trabsky, 'Counting the Dead During a Pandemic' in Carl Stychin (ed), *Law, Humanities and the Covid Crisis* (University of London Press, 2023).

1

Legal Epistemologies of Death

Introduction

The average life expectancy of a British adult has dropped by at least 13 months since 2015. Researchers blame widespread cuts to healthcare and welfare spending, spiralling costs of living, and increases in dementia, diabetes, and cancer diagnoses.[1] This trend doesn't even include the deterioration of mortality during the recent global pandemic, which appears to have decreased life expectancy, particularly in already disadvantaged communities, not only in the United Kingdom but also throughout Europe, the United States, and elsewhere. The facile truism that every generation will live longer than the previous one has been thoroughly debunked. The reversal in life expectancy, or more specifically how it disrupts the fantastical human desire for immortality, reveals a great deal about transformations to the epistemology of death in the twenty-first century. Death is understood today as something that can be mastered, controlled, and manipulated. Governments can put an individual to death by their own hands or through their complicity with others. They often let vulnerable populations die by failing to provide timely medical, social, or legal assistance. They also extend the lives of the most advantaged in society by financing technologies that can only be accessed by the few. Governments routinely invest in the management of life to a point where they allow individuals to die. The recent deterioration in life expectancy is not a catastrophe for the state; on the contrary, it is a problem to be monitored, quantified, and calculated. Whether they create the conditions to edge death ever slightly closer or whether they remain indifferent to the fatal consequences of their

---

1 See Denis Campbell, 'Rise in life expectancy has stalled since 2010, research shows', *Guardian*, 18 July 2017 <www.theguardian.com/society/2017/jul/18/rise-in-life-expectancy-has-stalled-since-2010-research-shows>; Patrick Collinson, 'Life expectancy falls by six months in biggest drop in UK forecasts', *Guardian*, 8 March 2019 <www.theguardian.com/society/2019/mar/07/life-expectancy-slumps-by-five-months>.

DOI: 10.4324/9781003222163-1

decision-making, it is without doubt that in seeking mastery over the vicissitudes of mortality, governments reify the value of death.

In 2022, *The Lancet*, a prominent medical journal, published a wide-ranging report on the paradox of dying in the twenty-first century. The report contends that dying is unbalanced across the world, death has lost its value for society, and vulnerable populations suffer greatly from a lack of investment in end-of-life care. Many people die of preventable conditions, particularly in low-income countries, and they die without access to affordable and timely medical treatment. In contrast, dying in high-income countries is often a protracted process, where "[f]utile or potentially inappropriate treatment can continue into the last hours of life".[2] Ineffectual medical treatment can be a major cause of health poverty for the survivors of the deceased, contribute to needless suffering for the dying person and their family, and divert indispensable funding from palliative care, which has the potential to improve the quality of dying in the final moments of life. The report exhorts governments to not only recognise the 'value' of death but also to reform institutional death systems to restore equality to the dying process. But to do so they first need to critique the teleological fantasy that they can master death, that science can manipulate death by forever extending life, and mortality, much like nature, is an obstacle to be tamed through technology.

While the *Lancet* report makes a timely intervention into changing societal attitudes towards death in the twenty-first century, it is a misnomer to claim that governments fail to recognise the value of death. This book begins with the polemic that states have always comprehended death as 'valuable', by which I mean that they make sense of death through the lens of economic rationality. In *Undoing the Demos: Neoliberalism's Stealth Revolution*, Wendy Brown traces how life has become governed by neoliberal reason, which "takes shape as a governing rationality extending a specific formulation of economic values, practices, and metrics to every dimension of human life".[3] Although neoliberalism has become a catchphrase for the privatisation of public goods, corporatisation of government services, and financialisation of human capital, its uniqueness lies in how techniques of economisation can be extended into all spheres of human activity, and how the application of these techniques do not necessarily involve the monetisation of those spheres. Brown charts the extent to which the economisation of life, whether in the domains of justice, work, education, or the household, involves subjugating all experiences to the *"model of the market . . .*

---

2 'Report of the *Lancet* Commission on the Value of Death: Bringing Death Back into Life' (2022) 399 *Lancet* 837, 837.

3 Wendy Brown, *Undoing the Demos: Neoliberalism's Stealth Revolution* (Zone Books, 2015) 30.

even where money is not an issue", and construing all "human beings exhaustively as market actors, always, only, and everywhere as *homo oeconomicus*".[4]

The economisation of death is a key theme of *Death: New Trajectories of Law*, which is comprehensively explored in Chapter 2 but reverberates in different forms in Chapters 3 and 4. The important intervention that this book makes by contending that death has become subject to a governing logic of economisation is that this wouldn't have been possible without the complicity of legal institutions. Laws are depicted in each chapter as enabling, if not extending, the concept of economy into domains which were perhaps at one point in time never thought of as primarily economic. It is without doubt that funeral industries were established long before the twenty-first century, a point made by John Troyer in his history of the invention of embalming towards the end of the American Civil War.[5] And lucrative markets for the trafficking of dead bodies, especially of Indigenous and African American remains, to medical schools throughout the British Empire were legalised by governments in the eighteenth and nineteenth centuries.[6] However, the acceleration of biotechnological innovation in the second half of the twentieth century, the way that technology has transformed medical epistemologies of death, and the consequential changes in law to definitions of death, counting of the dead, and knowledge of the corpse, have all contributed to the economisation of death in the twenty-first century. This confluence of medicine, law, and technology has not simply transformed legal relations between life and death, but also, it has revealed how the governance of death is increasingly inextricable from economic rationality.

Death: New Trajectories in Law examines how legal institutions reify the value of death in the twenty-first century. Its starting point is that biotechnological innovations have extended life to such an extent that death has become an epistemological problem for legal institutions. Chapter 2 explores how legal definitions of death, which were developed in response to advances in life-supporting technology, are subject to the governing logic of economisation. Chapter 3 shows how legal technologies for registering a death, which normalise death as an inevitable outcome of life, reshape what kind of deaths are counted during a pandemic. Chapter 4 investigates how technologies for

---

4 Ibid 31 (emphasis in original).
5 John Troyer, *Technologies of the Human Corpse* (MIT Press, 2020).
6 See, eg, Ruth Richardson, *Death, Dissection and the Destitute* (University of Chicago Press, 2001); Michael Sappol, *A Traffic of Dead Bodies: Anatomy and Embodied Social Identity in Nineteenth-Century America* (Princeton University Press, 2004); Helen Mac-Donald, *Possessing the Dead: The Artful Science of Anatomy* (Melbourne University Press, 2010).

recycling cadaveric tissue, which dissect the body into lucrative waste, problematise the legal status of the corpse. The question that unites each chapter is how legal institutions respond to technologies that bring death before their laws. The book argues for an interdisciplinary approach, informed by the writings of Georges Bataille, Wendy Brown, Georges Canguilhem, and Michel Foucault, to understand how legal epistemologies are increasingly disrupted, challenged, and countered by technologies that repurpose death to extend, nourish, and foster human life. It contends that legal theorists and social scientists need to rethink doctrinal perspectives of law when theorising how law defines the moment of death, shapes what kind of deaths count, and recycles the debris of the dead.

The aim of this book is to show how doctrinal approaches to understanding law are unable to account for how legal institutions recognise the value of death in the world. Inventions in surgical methods and treatments, pharmaceutical drugs, and life-supporting technology since the middle of the twentieth century have prompted legal decision-makers to define death in new ways, which suffuse knowledge of the moment of death with discourses of economic rationality. Transformations in classification systems for death causation, which underpin the technology of death registration, have challenged the way that deaths are counted by legal institutions. Bureaucratic procedures for registering a death metamorphose a singular life into valuable statistics for constructing a normal amount of death in any given population. The development of lucrative markets for the recycling of cadaveric tissue have unsettled doctrinal perspectives of the legal status of the corpse. They have done so by recognising the value of dissecting the corpse into infinitesimal units of waste that can be repurposed for human consumption. This book thus offers a 'new trajectory in law' by rethinking how death can be conceptualised in the legal discipline. Before I embark on this trajectory, it is necessary to highlight two concepts, *thanato-politics* and *normalisation*, that are important for comprehending how death is governed by law in the twenty-first century.

Thanato-politics

In the final part of the first volume of *The History of Sexuality*, Michel Foucault offers a strident critique of the transformations in the governance of life and death in the eighteenth and nineteenth centuries. He marks this epoch as a turning point between the decline of sovereign power and the emergence of bio-power in the West. While Foucault concedes that human life, as an object of power-knowledge relations, had always been exploited by sovereigns, particularly when expanding their territories, sentencing an enemy to death, or quarantining plague towns, since at least the eighteenth century, humankind began problematising

> what it meant to be a living species in a living world, to have a body, conditions of existence, probabilities of life, an individual and collective welfare, forces that could be modified, and a space in which they could be distributed in an optimal manner.[7]

In other words, life became an object of knowledge, and through the development of human sciences, life was dissected into microscopic components to be observed, quantified, and manipulated. Insofar as these sciences transfixed humankind, life became a problem for governments, which entailed developing a range of political technologies for managing the vicissitudes of life and death.

Foucault explains in *The History of Sexuality* that an analytics of bio-power consists of a collection of political technologies. This includes an *anatomo-politics* of the human body and a *bio-politics* of the population. The former refers to the individualisation of the subject, and the subjugation and docility of the body through practices of examination, discipline, and surveillance, whereas the latter takes as its site of intervention not the individual subject but the population, the 'species body', or human life itself. Bio-power differs from older forms of power insofar as it seeks to incite, control, and optimise life. It also involves the delegation of authority from state institutions and the distribution of power-knowledge relations into every facet of life, from households to schools and from markets to clinics. "Power is everywhere", writes Foucault, "not because it embraces everything, but because it comes from everywhere".[8] In the decentralisation of power and knowledge, a population emerges as both an object of scientific study and a problem to be managed by governments. Foucault makes it clear, however, that sovereignty is not replaced by bio-power, whether disciplinary or regulatory, but rather revalorised through practices of government that intervene directly and indirectly in the administration of a population. While the modern incantation of bio-power greatly differs from sovereign power – which was overwhelmingly dominated by the spectacle of law's violence – it only does so by reshaping a 'deductive' power over life and death into a 'positive' power to foster, elongate, and maximise life.

This does not imply, though, that death was no longer of interest to states in the eighteenth and nineteenth centuries. Death appears as a contradictory figure in *The History of Sexuality*, where it is simultaneously

---

7 Michel Foucault, *The History of Sexuality, Volume 1: The Will to Knowledge*, tr Robert Hurley (Penguin Books, 1998) 142.
8 Ibid 93.

a remainder of the splendour of the sovereign's power to put someone to death while also being a limit point of the exercise of bio-power that seeks to elongate life. It even manifests at times in Foucault's writing as a moment of absolute resistance to the concentration of power in the state. Indeed, in *Society Must Be Defended* Foucault remarks that "[p]ower no longer recognizes death, power literally ignores death".[9] He also contrasts death to mortality, the latter of which power can control, and surmises that "power has a grip on [death] only in general, overall or statistical terms".[10] While I will turn to the statistical value of mortality in Chapter 3, it will suffice to observe that these terse quotes do not give a full account of Foucault's theory of death. It is without doubt that the sovereign's "right to *take* a life or *let* live" was replaced in the eighteenth century by "a power that exerts a positive influence on life, that endeavours to administer, optimise, and multiply it, subjecting it to precise controls and comprehensive regulations".[11] However, this book argues that death was never ignored by power in the eighteenth century, it did not vanish from its grasp in the nineteenth century, and it was not repressed in the twentieth century when bio-power flourished as a dominant arrangement of government. In later writings, Foucault precisely coins the term *thanato-politics* to account for how political technologies for managing death appeared alongside, intertwined with, and immanent to the governance of life in the modern era.[12]

Thanato-politics is conceptually different to *necro-politics*, which has been widely mobilised across the humanities and social sciences over the last decade.[13] The latter appears in Achille Mbembe's writings as either the opposite, underside, or an extension of bio-power. "I have demonstrated", Mbembe writes in *Necro-politics*, "that the notion of biopower is insufficient to account for contemporary forms of

---

9 Michel Foucault, *Society Must Be Defended: Lectures at the Collège de France, 1975– 1976*, tr David Macey (Picador, 2003) 248.

10 Ibid.

11 Foucault (n 7) 136–137 (emphasis in original).

12 Michel Foucault, 'The Political Technology of Individuals' in Luther H Martin, Huck Gutman and Patrick H Hutton (eds), *Technologies of the Self: A Seminar with Michel Foucault* (University of Massachusetts Press, 1988) 160.

13 See, eg, R Guy Emerson, *Necropolitics: Living Death in Mexico* (Palgrave Macmillan, 2019); Ariadna Estévez (ed.), *Necropower in North America: The Legal Spatialization of Disposability and Lucrative Death* (Palgrave Macmillan, 2021); Francisco Ferrándiz and Antonius C G M Robben (eds), *Necropolitics: Mass Graves and Exhumations in the Age of Human Rights* (University of Pennsylvania Press, 2015); Jin Haritaworn, Adi Kuntsman and Silvia Posocco (eds), *Queer Necropolitics* (Routledge, 2014); Jasbir K Puar, *Terrorist Assemblages: Homonationalism in Queer Times* (Duke University Press, 2007); C L Quinan and Kathrin Thiele (eds), *Biopolitics, Necropolitics, Cosmopolitics* (Routledge, 2021); Jothie Rajah, *Discounting Life: Necropolitical Law, Culture, and the Long War on Terror* (Cambridge University Press, 2023); Christophe D Ringer, *Necropolitics: The Religious Crisis of Mass Incarceration in America* (Lexington Books, 2021).

the subjugation of life to the power of death".[14] He utilises the concept to describe how governments exercise sovereignty over life through the power of death – they decide who lives, who dies, and who to expose to violence – particularly in the context of slavery, occupation, colonisation, war, and genocide. Mbembe is indebted to the work of philosopher Giorgio Agamben in focusing on how the state of exception normalises the sovereign's right to kill. He puts forward the concept of *necro-politics* to explain how

> in our contemporary world, weapons are deployed in the interest of maximally destroying persons and creating *death-worlds*, that is, new and unique forms of social existence in which vast populations are subjected to living conditions that confer upon them the status of the *living dead*.[15]

In other words, necro-power can explain much better than an analytics of bio-power how governments can exercise a 'right' to kill individuals, mutilate and disfigure populations, and, particularly through cultivating and disseminating discourses of racism, how they can create the conditions for social or political death in the twenty-first century.

In comparison to this reformulation of sovereign power, *thanato-politics* is quotidian in its distribution throughout a population. In Foucault's writings it is not the antithesis of *bio-politics* but the continuity of its techniques in another direction of life. If it is agreed that death is not repressed, ignored, or banished by state institutions – a point I make in my previous writings[16] – then the experience of dying and the afterlife of the corpse are as much a part of an analytics of bio-power as every other facet of life. This perhaps explains why Foucault is at pains to emphasise how the sovereign's power "to *take* life or *let* live" is transformed in contemporary times into "a power to *foster* life or *disallow* it to the point of death".[17] To put this differently, if *bio-politics* describes the way that governments invest in life, foster it, and manage its fluctuations, *thanato-politics* denotes the techniques by which governments facilitate or resist death, tolerate or prolong it, or monitor, control, and manipulate its trends. In this book, then, *thanato-politics* is not a description of how governments subjugate human beings to terror, violence, or death. Instead, it is a conceptual tool to give an account of how a panoply of institutions harness technologies to allow individuals to die.

14 Achille Mbembe, *Necro-Politics*, tr Steven Corcoran (Duke University Press, 2019) 92.
15 Ibid (emphasis in original).
16 Marc Trabsky, *Law and the Dead: Technology, Relations and Institutions* (Routledge, 2019).
17 Foucault (n 7) 138 (emphasis in original).

This interpretation of *thanato-politics* is more akin to Lauren Berlant's theory of 'slow death' than Mbembe's description of *necro-politics*. In an essay on causality, subjectivity, and the purported 'obesity epidemic', Berlant defines 'slow death' as "the physical wearing out of a population and the deterioration of people in that population that is very nearly a defining condition of their experience and historical existence".[18] Due to Berlant's interests in how the exercise of bio-power creates knowledges of health and subjects individuals to techniques of normalisation, 'letting die' is not a passive abandonment of life but an active management of the circulation of life and death. My theorisation of *thanato-politics* in this book differs from Berlant's concept of 'slow death' in several instances. First, I mobilise the concept to describe how legal institutions in particular harness technologies to allow individuals to die. But second, the term enables me to show how in allowing individuals to die, legal institutions reify the value of death in the world, which is to say they economise the *allowance* of a specific amount of death in any given population. The contrasts I am drawing here between *thanato-politics* and *necro-politics* are not intended to introduce a hierarchy of concepts. I suggest that both political technologies are theoretically useful for describing how sovereign power and bio-power function, sometimes inextricably, while other times almost separably, in different parts of the world. However, if it is agreed that the potency of sovereign power waned in the eighteenth century, rather than insist on its revival in the form of a totalising power that subjugates life to (social) death, I contend that it was reshaped by bio-power into *a* political technology for 'taking life or letting live'. In other words, I suggest that *necro-politics* is one tool amongst others, available to both state and non-state institutions in the governance of death, whether those deaths are violent or accidental, or expected or sudden. *Thanato-politics* is presented in this book as another technology of bio-power, however, one that is mobilised by legal institutions in subjecting death to the governing logic of economisation.

Normalisation

It is not only death that affects Foucault in the final part of *The History of Sexuality*. In the pages following his ruminations on the governance of death in the eighteenth century, he sketches out a theory of law, which since its publication has generated much confusion in the legal discipline. Foucault explicitly states that law and its institutions did not vanish with the emergence of the age of bio-power. However, he also insists

---

18 Lauren Berlant, 'Slow Death (Sovereignty, Obesity, Lateral Agency)' (2007) 33(4) *Critical Inquiry* 754.

that law is increasingly functioning as a norm, and legal institutions, mechanisms, and technologies form part of a 'continuum of regulatory apparatuses'. "This argument for the co-existence, hybridization and mutual inter-dependence of law and norm in societies where government takes the form of the calculated administration of life", write Nikolas Rose and Mariana Valverde, "may surprise those who think that Foucault denied the role of law and legal mechanisms in the exercise of modern forms of power".[19] Indeed, many legal scholars have interpreted Foucault's claim that law has been replaced by the norm as an indication that the former's significance has declined in contemporary life. This line of argument goes on to claim that Foucault erroneously categorises law with sovereign power and neglects to comprehend the local specificities of the force of legal institutions, technologies, and relations.

In 'Norms, Discipline, and the Law', François Ewald unapologetically redeems the function of legal institutions in Foucault's writings. He claims that far from marginalising the status of law or removing it from an analytics of bio-power, Foucault seeks in *The History of Sexuality* to understand how legal institutions, technologies, and mechanisms became reshaped in the modern era. While law is not isomorphic with the norm, Foucault questions, according to Ewald, how law operates alongside or intertwined with a governance of life and death in a 'normalizing society':

> His further commentary makes it clear that the formation of a normalizing society in no way diminished the power of law or caused judicial institutions to disappear. In fact, normalization tends to be accompanied by an astonishing proliferation of legislation. Practically speaking, legislators never expressed themselves as freely or as extensively as in the age of bio-power. The norm, then, is opposed not to law itself but to what Foucault would call 'the juridical': the institution of law as the expression of a sovereign's power.[20]

Misunderstandings of Foucault's writings have tended to suggest that law has lost some kind of essential characteristic, which in the transformation from sovereign to bio-power has been replaced with the norm. However, Foucault does not suggest that the sovereign functioning of law was completely superseded with a regulatory orientation. Rather he simply contends that "law operates more and more as a norm".[21]

19 Nikolas Rose and Mariana Valverde, 'Governed by Law?' (1998) 7(4) *Social & Legal Studies* 541, 542.
20 François Ewald, 'Norms, Discipline, and the Law' (tr Marjorie Beale) (1990) 30 *Representations* 138.
21 Foucault (n 7) 144.

What he means by this is law is increasingly organised as a technology of normalisation, and at once, harnesses normalising technologies in its functioning. Normalisation, according to Ewald, is a mechanism for the production of norms, standards, and rules:

> Normalization is a means of assigning value that renders absolute standards of perfection meaningless. The good is figured in terms of adequacy – the good product is adequate to the purpose it was meant to serve. Within the normative system, values are not defined a priori but instead through an endless process of comparison that is made possible by normalization.[22]

To put this differently, normalisation is one technique amongst many for disciplining bodies (*anatomo-politics*) and controlling populations (*bio-politics*), that is, for governing relations between life and death. It is a political technology that in the era of bio-power is indistinguishable from, but not isomorphic with, legal institutions, technologies, and mechanisms. This idea of normalisation as a technology that produces an outcome emerges from Ewald's interpretation of the norm as denoting "both a particular variety of rules, and a way of *producing* them and, perhaps most significantly of all, a principle of *valorisation*".[23] Yet Ewald also emphasises the necessity of distinguishing "between the norm itself and the apparatus, institution, or technique of power that brings it into action and functions according to its principles".[24] In this book, I heed Ewald's warning to not collapse law into the category of the norm. Indeed, I consider law as an arrangement that consists of institutions, technologies, and mechanisms, which together construct norms, deploy norms, and self-referentially, cultivate legal epistemologies through the principle of normalisation.

In previous writings, I conceived of law as a network of institutions, relations, and technologies. I utilised this conceptual framework to write a history of how coroners engaged with the dead and attached them to law in the nineteenth and twentieth centuries. In *Law and the Dead* I took aim at how a governance of death is theorised by Foucault as a *political* technology, insisting upon the specificity of law's institutional formations. In this book, I broaden my conceptualisation of law by categorising legal institutions as normalising insofar as they distribute law-making in more diverse forms, include non-legal claims to knowledge in their epistemologies, and anchor legal technologies in governmental practices. While the idea of the governance of death as both a

---

22 Ewald (n 20) 152.
23 Ibid 140 (my emphasis).
24 Ibid 153.

political and legal technology may be ill-suited to writing a history of the office of coroner in the nineteenth and twentieth centuries, the increasingly blurring of *anatomo-politics* and *bio-politics* in the twenty-first century has resulted in the entanglement of the political and the legal, or as Rose and Valverde say, the governmentalisation of law. This concept facilitates a critical analysis of how legal technologies are produced by and transform non-legal institutions, and how legal institutions deploy political technologies to produce wide-ranging effects in society.[25] The book thus builds upon a theory of normalisation to account for how legal institutions reify the value of death in the twenty-first century.

Trajectories

Medical innovations in the second half of the twentieth century extended life to such an extent that death became an epistemological problem for legal institutions. The inventions of medication, machinery, and surgical methods and treatments to prolong, sustain, and support life have problematised legal definitions of the moment of death. This has consequences for decision-making about when medical treatment can be lawfully withdrawn from a dying person, when organs and tissue can be extracted from a consenting donor, and when a death can be certified by medical practitioners for state-based registration systems. Human beings are living longer through their entanglements with machines, devices, and apparatuses, and the support of labour-intensive human resources. However, the scientific-technical mastery sought by legal, medical, and actuarial institutions on the moment of death has become increasingly contingent on the question of economic rationality. Knowledge of death, its temporality and spatiality, is not simply longed for by judges, clinicians, and insurers; it is also subject to the governing logic of economisation. Chapter 2 examines how legal definitions of death have become economised in the twenty-first century. It aims to account for how the figure Michel Foucault calls *homo oeconomicus* extends into domains of death, but also what the effects of economic rationality are for understanding transformations in the governance of death in the twenty-first century.

25 Rose and Valverde write that "an analysis of law from the perspective of government would turn away from the canonical texts and the privileged sites of legal reason, and turn towards the minor, the mundane, the grey, meticulous and detailed work of regulatory apparatuses . . . of all the places where, in the bureaucratic workings of our over-governed existence, laws, rules and standards shape our ways of going on, and all the little judges of conduct exercise their petty powers of adjudication and enforcement": Rose and Valverde (n 19) 546.

Governmental responses to global pandemics make use of an array of technologies for managing life, maximising its efficacy, and exploiting its vitality. In Chapter 3, I examine how death is registered during a pandemic and how each registration becomes enumerated in a statistical tabulation of mortality rates. Technologies of registration depend on the creation of universal nomenclature for ascertaining death causation, which excludes various circumstances of a life to stabilise a communicable disease as a normative category for classification. This means that the registration of a death is conditioned upon differentiating between the normal and the pathological, standards and variations, and an average and excess. The chapter reveals how the technology of registration can be harnessed to pathologise specific kinds of death while unproblematically reifying the concept of a normal death. It argues that pandemics expose the role that laws of registration perform in constructing a 'natural' state of the population. Registration is a normalising technology that is inextricable from how state institutions determine what deaths count.

Necro-waste designates the by-products of different applications of work on the corpse in death-related trades. It includes an ensemble of materials – fluids, gases, tissue, bone, skin, implants, chemicals, and effluence – discarded from post-mortem examinations, medical research and training, transplantation procedures, plastination techniques, and technologies for the disposal of dead bodies. Chapter 4 investigates how the recycling of cadaveric tissue problematises the legal status of the corpse as either a person or a thing. The legal doctrine of *res nullius*, which originated in the common law in the seventeenth century, is challenged in the twenty-first century by technologies that repurpose cadaveric tissue for a global market of medical devices, implants, treatments, and pharmaceuticals. The technologies involved in converting human remains into biomedical products both dissect the corpse into lucrative waste and signal its use-value for human consumption. They also invite an alternative perspective of knowing the corpse by revealing the dead body to be intrinsically excessive. The chapter rethinks legal epistemologies of the corpse through the discourse of lucrative necro-waste. More than the corpse itself, the recycling of cadaveric tissue reveals an excess of meaning, or as Georges Bataille writes, a general economy that haunts the debris of death.

Further Reading

- Berlant, Lauren, 'Slow Death (Sovereignty, Obesity, Lateral Agency)' (2007) 33(4) *Critical Inquiry* 754.
- Ewald, François, 'Norms, Discipline, and the Law' (tr Marjorie Beale) (1990) 30 *Representations* 138.

- Foucault, Michel, *The History of Sexuality, Volume 1: The Will to Knowledge*, tr Robert Hurley (Penguin Books, 1998).
- Foucault, Michel, *Society Must Be Defended: Lectures at the Collège de France, 1975–1976*, tr David Macey (Picador, 2003).
- Mbembe, Achille, *Necro-Politics*, tr Steven Corcoran (Duke University Press, 2019).
- Rose, Nikolas and Mariana Valverde, 'Governed by Law?' (1998) 7(4) *Social & Legal Studies* 541.

2

The Economisation
of Death

Introduction

In 2014, the World Health Organization (WHO) commissioned a technical expert report on developing universal standards for the determination of death.[1] The impetus for the commission was that since the mid-twentieth century, medical innovations have obfuscated epistemologies of death. Inventions in mechanical ventilation and cardiac support devices, and the emergence of intensive care units and cardiopulmonary resuscitation, have sustained life beyond the point where the heart ceases beating and the lungs stop breathing. The report surmises that diagnostic criteria for defining death vary around the world due to an imbalance in access to life-supporting technology. Even the conceptualisation of death as a continual process rather than an identifiable event differs widely between countries. This has legal ramifications on decision-making about when to lawfully withdraw life-support technology, such as ventilators, defibrillators, and feeding tubes, for persons who have already died.

The WHO report responds to these quandaries by developing universal guidelines for diagnosing death in a clinical setting. The guidelines contain standardised workflows or checklists for determining the precise moment of death. The first workflow describes the irreversible cessation of cardiopulmonary function, which has been the most common classification of death since at least the nineteenth century. However, due to the invention of cardiac support devices, which can reanimate the heart and extend life for those with cardiopulmonary failure, the second workflow depicts the irreversible cessation of neurological function. The language of 'brain death' emerged as a diagnostic criterion for defining death in the late 1960s, and it enables medical practitioners to withdraw life-supporting technology for persons with severe brain injury, who without

---

1 World Health Organization, *Clinical Criteria for the Determination of Death: WHO Technical Expert Consultation, 22–23 September 2014* (World Health Organization, 2017).

DOI: 10.4324/9781003222163-2

such interventions would be declared dead. While each checklist provides different steps for determining either the irreversible cessation of cardio-pulmonary or neurological function, they both have the same endpoint of death.

Pivotal to decision-making in a clinical setting is a medical judgment about when to cease providing 'unnecessary' treatment or when to with-draw life-supporting technology from a dying person. In other words, a clinician can determine the moment of death by not attempting cardio-pulmonary resuscitation, or by removing the ventilators, defibrillators, or feeding tubes that are keeping the person alive. The circulatory logic of this criterion – that is, death is diagnosed by allowing a person to die – is main-tained by the lack of definition in the WHO report of what kind of judg-ment is involved in deciding when "treatment has become unnecessary".[2] While the guidelines leave 'medical judgment' indeterminate, they seek to embed temporality into clinical practices for classifying death. For death only makes sense as the endpoint of a checklist of steps and tests when conceptualised in relation to the rationalisation of time. Thus, any diagno-sis must only be made after a moment of delay, whether that may be two or five minutes, to see if cardiopulmonary or neurological functions spon-taneously return. What is at stake here is not only the travesty of misdiag-nosing death when a person is alive but also the unnecessary expenditure of scarce medical resources on persons who have already died.

Medical innovations in the second half of the twentieth century extended life to such an extent that death became an epistemological problem for legal institutions. The inventions of medication, machinery, and surgical methods and treatments to prolong, sustain, and support life have problematised legal definitions of the moment of death. This has consequences for decision-making about when medical treatment can be lawfully withdrawn from a dying person, when organs and tissue can be extracted from a consenting donor, and when a death can be certified by medical practitioners for state-based registration systems. Human beings are living longer through their entanglements with machines, devices, and apparatuses, and the support of labour-intensive human resources. However, the scientific-technical mastery sought by legal, medical, and actuarial institutions on the moment of death has become increasingly contingent on the question of economic rationality. Knowl-edge of death, its temporality and spatiality, is not simply longed for by judges, clinicians, and insurers; it is also subject to the governing logic of economisation. This is part of a repertoire of institutional practices

---

2 Ibid 5. In the 2012 forum that preceded the 2014 report, death was defined as "[t]he moment in time during the dying process when the individual passes from the state of being alive to that of being dead": Sam Shemie, et al., 'International Guideline Develop-ment for the Determination of Death' (2014) 40 *Intensive Care Medicine* 788, 790.

that seek to economise many aspects of mortality, ranging from the disposal of human remains; management of estates and the inheritance of debt; provision of social, psychological, and spiritual services for the bereaved; and medical, financial, and legal advice for the dying.

This chapter examines how legal definitions of death have become economised in the twenty-first century. The twentieth century witnessed a transformation from locating death in the absence of breath or the lack of a heartbeat to neurological concepts of 'brain death', the diagnosis of which remains the responsibility of medical professionals. The orientation towards a neurological definition of death emerged through law reform processes, where discussions about when medical treatment for persons with severe brain damage can be lawfully withdrawn were interpreted through the economic frameworks of resource allocations, cost-benefit calculations, and supply and demand. If a condition of possibility of human life in the twenty-first century is a historically specific form of economic rationality, which extols human beings to optimise the economic value of death, then this chapter explores how a legal determination of death is inextricable from economisation. It aims to account for how the figure Michel Foucault calls *homo oeconomicus* extends into domains of death, but also what the effects of neoliberal rationality are for understanding transformations in the governance of death in the twenty-first century.[3]

Defining Death

The invention of the iron lung problematised medical definitions of death in the twentieth century. Developed by Philip Drinker and Louis Shaw in 1928 to stimulate breathing in persons with respiratory failure, the iron lung was initially deployed to remedy coal gas poisoning. By the 1930s the device became widely used to treat sufferers of poliomyelitis, and it resulted in reducing the case fatality rate of the highly infectious disease. Prior to the invention of the iron lung and a range of medical devices for visualising the interiority of the body, death was self-evidently diagnosed by clinicians as the cessation of respiration or circulation. The time of death was to be perceived visually, auditorily, and tactilely, and medical practitioners seldom owned a monopoly on all of the methods for testing for the signs of death (although the use

---

3   I have previously examined how economic rationality suffuses legal relations between the living, the dying and the state in legislative regimes for voluntary assisted dying: Marc Trabsky, 'The Neoliberal Rationality of Voluntary Assisted Dying' in Daniel J Fleming and David J Carter (eds), *Voluntary Assisted Dying: Law? Health? Justice?* (ANU University Press, 2022) 95–111. Chapter 2 builds upon that initial work by deploying a theory of economisation to account for transformations in legal definitions of death.

of the stethoscope aptly signified their importance in the trade). Rudimentary tools included holding a mirror under a person's nose to check whether they were still breathing, in which case the mirror would fog up; using stimuli, such as smelling salts, to wake up what was presumed to be a slumbering body; or simply sitting around the corpse to wait for the stench of putrefaction to inundate the environment. The iron lung disrupted these clinical practices because it could mechanically facilitate respiration in individuals who in previous centuries would already have been declared dead due to the absence of breath or a pulse.

With the widespread dissemination of the iron lung, death could no longer simply be defined by the cessation of respiration or circulation. When human beings with respiratory paralysis were living inside these machines for years, and sometimes for the remainder of their lives, the medical profession was faced with the possibility that it had to rethink its knowledge of death.[4] The original 'Drinker respirator' inspired clinicians in Denmark, Australia, and the United Kingdom to invent more robust and less costly devices due to an insatiable demand for mechanical ventilation to treat polio sufferers. The effects of the increased demand only improved the efficacy of the iron lung, which by the 1940s was used to transform a fatal prognosis of diaphragm paralysis into a brief sojourn inside a negative pressure ventilator. The popularity of the device only waned in the 1950s with the near eradication of polio through the administration of vaccines and the invention of the artificial positive pressure ventilator.

Also known as the modern ventilator, it replaced the iron lung as the primary means to support a person with respiratory failure, because it more efficiently stimulated breathing, and provided oxygen directly into the lungs. The ventilator emerged alongside a raft of technological developments in the second half of the twentieth century, such as the establishment of intensive care units in hospitals and the development of cardiopulmonary resuscitation first aid; the invention of cardiac pacemakers, defibrillators, and other support devices, which when implanted or attached to a person could stimulate the heart to pump blood even in the face of cardiopulmonary failure; and the formulation of surgical methods and immunosuppressive drugs for successfully transplanting kidneys, livers, lungs, and hearts from dead cadavers into living recipients. All these biotechnological innovations were designed to prolong, sustain, and support life for a human being who at the turn of the twentieth century would have been declared dead due to the absence of

---

4 See the story of Frederick Snite, Jr, who lived mostly inside an iron lung in the United States from 1936 to 1954, in Gini Laurie, 'Ventilator Users, Home Care, and Independent Living: A Historical Perspective' in Irene S Gilgoff (ed.), *Breath of Life: The Role of the Ventilator in Managing Life-Threatening Illnesses* (Scarecrow Press, 2002) 162.

breath or the lack of a heartbeat. The use of pioneering machines, devices, and apparatuses, as well as inventive surgical methods and treatments, to keep the 'near-dead patient' alive led to calls in the late 1960s for a new medical definition of death.

The 'living cadaver' first appeared in medical lexicon as a taxonomy for the corporeal state of being wholly dependent for respiration, circulation, and alimentation on life-support machines. The term depicted a person who was living in a state of irreversible unconsciousness (*coma dépassé*) and who without the sustenance of ventilators, defibrillators, and feeding tubes to stimulate the lungs, heart, and gastrointestinal tract would be diagnosed as dead. To embody the 'living cadaver', as the medical anthropologist Margaret Lock puts it, was to possess a dead brain but an alive body; it was to be "betwixt and between, both alive and dead".[5] This liminal state of corporeality problematised different aspects of the common law in the 1960s. First, it challenged the presumed neutrality of legal institutions, which for centuries shied away from providing a legal definition of death and instead maintained that "the moment of a person's death [was] a question of fact for determination at trial on the basis of expert testimony".[6] In other words, the mere appearance of the living cadaver challenged legal institutions to codify a definition of death. Second, it threw into doubt long-standing norms about when medical treatment could be lawfully withdrawn from a person who had a brain injury, and a body that was alive due to support from machines, devices, and apparatuses. Third, it disrupted a range of legal events that could only proceed from the point where a medical practitioner declares a person dead. In short, the living cadaver posed an epistemological problem for how medical institutions understand their legal duties towards taking care of a near-dead patient, and for how legal institutions know when a person becomes a corpse for the purposes of initiating a coronial investigation, signing a death certificate, reading a will, claiming a benefit from a financial, legal, or social institution, burying or cremating remains, and prior to all of that, consenting to the removal of organs or tissue for transplantation. The legal consequences of the 'near-dead patient' or the 'living cadaver', which only appeared with innovations in life-supporting technology, led to calls for reform

---

5 Margaret Lock, 'On Dying Twice: Culture, Technology and the Determination of Death' in Margaret Lock, Alan Young and Alberto Cambrosio (eds), *Living and Working with the New Medical Technologies: Intersections of Inquiry* (Cambridge University Press, 2000) 233. See also, Margaret Lock, *Twice Dead: Organ Transplants and the Reinvention of Death* (University of California Press, 2002).

6 Russell Gordon Smith, 'Refining the Definition of Death for Australian Legislation' (1983) 14 *Melbourne University Law Review* 199, 212. Smith quotes Mr Justice Fullager, who was then a barrister, but later became a judge, commenting in 1965 that "the Courts have not, and will not, lay down any rule as to when a man is dead".

of whether death should be defined in law, and if so, how the definition should be constructed.

In 1968, an Ad Hoc Committee of Harvard Medical School, which was chaired by the anaesthesiologist Henry Knowles Beecher and consisted of clinicians, ethicists, and philosophers, answered those calls by recommending the creation of a new legal definition of death.[7] This definition, which was named 'brain death', introduced for the first time an 'irreversible cessation of neurological function' as a criterion for diagnosing death. The Harvard Ad Hoc Committee first argued that brain death was the most efficient way to resolve the problem of how to determine when a person had died in the situation where their brain was irreversibly damaged, but their body was kept alive through its entanglements with ventilators, defibrillators, and feeding tubes. Indeed, they claimed that only a new legal definition would provide clinicians, hospitals, courts, and families with certainty that removing life-support technology from a person in an irreversible coma would not result in criminal or civil liability. The second reason that the committee lobbied for a new definition of death was that it could hopefully put an end to debates of whether hospitals could lawfully obtain organs for transplantation from 'brain-dead' patients who still had a beating heart.

The Harvard Ad Hoc Committee formed towards the end of a decade that witnessed radical transformations in the medical science of transplantation. The 1960s saw the finessing of surgical procedures and invention of immunosuppressants for the efficacious transplantation of kidneys, livers, and hearts from dead donors. The speed at which surgeons developed ingenious techniques for relocating first a kidney but eventually a heart from a donated corpse to a living recipient was not immediately met by changes in law. The presumed legal requirement in the 1960s when Drs Guy Alexandre, James Hardy, Christiaan Barnard, and others experimented with transplantation procedures was that the donor must be declared legally dead before their organs can be removed. And yet, the only criterion that these surgeons had at their disposal to diagnose whether a donor was *factually* dead was the cessation of cardiopulmonary functions, which had to be applied in every case, even where donors were kept alive through their attachment to life-support technology. The 'dead donor rule', which gave assurances to the dying that they will not be prematurely 'made' dead for the purposes of retrieving their 'live' organs, and to the surgeons that they will not be charged with homicide when lawfully removing organs from a recently declared

---

7 Ad Hoc Committee of the Harvard Medical School, 'A Definition of Irreversible Coma: Report of the Ad Hoc Committee of the Harvard Medical School to Examine the Definition of Brain Death' (1968) 205(6) *Journal of the American Medical Association* 337.

corpse, did not provide much guidance for how hospitals should take care of 'living cadavers' or the 'brain dead'.

The dead donor rule was first enshrined in legislation in the United States in the *Uniform Anatomical Gift Act* (1968). The Act was consistently adopted by all 50 states, and it set out a legal framework for how donors could provide consent during their lives to the removal of their organs upon their death. The practical problem though with the dead donor rule, which the Harvard Ad Hoc Committee was set up to discuss, was that the death of a donor damages the viability of their organs for the purpose of transplantation. "Cell degeneration begins quickly after death", as Norman Cantor explains, "[e]ven if a dead donor's body is refrigerated, eyes must be removed within two hours of death; bones and heart valves within four hours; and blood vessels within six hours".[8] In other words, organs need to be removed immediately from a donor's body upon their death, and any delays to the retrieval of an organ risks damaging its capabilities for transplantation. Even then, the efficacy of organ transplantation can only be guaranteed by retrieving an organ from a heart-beating donor, which is to say, a donor who is in an 'irreversible coma', and through their connection to life-support technology possesses a beating heart.

Waiting too long, then, after a donor is legally declared dead to retrieve their organs risked damaging their viability for transplantation, while removing them from a living cadaver or the brain dead in the late 1960s would have contravened the law of homicide. Or as Cantor puts it, "[t]he problem was that an organ could be transplanted legally only after death had occurred, yet mechanical maintenance of heartbeat and breathing obstructed a declaration of death during the time that transplantable organs were still usable".[9] When the science of transplantation created an insatiable demand for organs that by the end of the decade had clearly outstripped supply, and the brain dead were increasingly lying in hospital beds across the United States thanks to developments in life-support technology, the Harvard Ad Hoc Committee decided that the most efficient way to facilitate organ procurement was by changing how law defines death. The economic discourse of supply and demand had a profound effect on the committee's decision to adopt an irreversible cessation of neurological function as a new definition of death in 1968.

Throughout the 1980s legal definitions of death were codified in many countries around the world. The idea that death could only be determined by testing for the absence of breath or the lack of a heartbeat was gradually replaced by legislative definitions of death as the "irreversible cessation of circulatory and respiratory functions" (cardiopulmonary death) or "irreversible cessation of all functions of the

---

8   Norman L Cantor, *After We Die: The Life and Times of the Human Cadaver* (Georgetown University Press, 2010) 17.

9   Ibid.

entire brain, including the brain stem" (neurological death).[10] This was first codified in the United States in 1981 in the *Uniform Declaration of Death Act*. It was then enacted in other jurisdictions with subtle changes to language that varied between each country. For example, in Australia, the *Human Tissue Act 1982* (Vic) s 41 defines death as the "irreversible cessation of circulation of blood in the body of the person; or irreversible cessation of all function of the brain of the person". While the language may differ between each jurisdiction, all agreed that neurological death is the cessation of *all* functions of the brain, particularly the brain stem, and the criteria and process for diagnosing death should be determined by the medical profession in accordance with recognised medical norms.[11] Hence, clinical guidelines for diagnosing brain death, such as those debated by the WHO Technical Expert Consultation in 2014, may diverge between each state, territory, and country.[12]

The United Kingdom is a case in point, for it has not codified a definition of death in legislation, but rather since the 1990s, has developed case law on when medical treatment can be lawfully withdrawn for a person in a persistent vegetative state. While brain death is medically different from a persistent vegetative state, the concern with liability for withdrawing treatment unlawfully, which inspired the actions of the Harvard Ad Hoc Committee, has been an impetus for cultivating a common law doctrine of how to define the moment of death. In *Airedale National Health Service Trust v Bland*, where a hospital applied to the court for a declaration that they could lawfully withdraw medical treatment for a patient who was in a persistent vegetative state for three and a half years, death was defined as the irreversible cessation of neurological function:

[t]his is because, as a result of developments in modern medical technology, doctors no longer associate death exclusively with breathing

10 This quote is from section 1 of the *Uniform Determination of Death Act 1981* (US). The language used in the legislation was endorsed by the President's Commission for the Study of Ethical Problems in Medicine and Biomedical and Behavioral Research, *Defining Death: A Report on the Medical, Legal and Ethical Issues in the Determination of Death* (US Government Printing Office, 1981).

11 The *Uniform Determination of Death Act* (1981) explicitly states that "A determination of death must be made in accordance with accepted medical standards". Most Australian states adopted similar language following a report of the Australian Law Reform Commission in 1977, which recommended the enactment of the Ad Hoc Committee of the Harvard Medical School's definition of death: Australian Law Reform Commission, *Human Tissue Transplants: Report No. 7* (Australian Government Printing Service, 1977).

12 See further, Task Force on Death and Dying, Institute of Society, Ethics and the Life Sciences, 'Refinements in Criteria for the Determination of Death: An Appraisal' (1972) 221 *Journal of the American Medical Association* 48, and President's Council on Bioethics, *Controversies in the Determination of Death: A White Paper of the President's Council on Bioethics* (President's Council on Bioethics, 2008).

and heart beat, and it has come to be accepted that death occurs when the brain, and in particular the brain stem, has been destroyed.[13]

Thus, even where the Harvard Ad Hoc Committee's definition of brain death has not been codified in legislation, courts have developed common law doctrine that recognises death as the irreversible cessation of all functions of the brain.

It has recently been pointed out in legal scholarship that the definition of brain death is a legal fiction or a social construct.[14] The concept has been consistently debated in legal, medical, and bioethical circles, whether in terms of its inconsistent use in clinical settings, indeterminate deployment in courts of law, or detachment from the realities of death as a prolonged affair. In these discussions there is an ongoing debate about whether the definition denotes death of the entire brain or whether it only means the upper (neocortical function) or lower part (brain stem function), and whether death is a continuous process or an identifiable event in time and space. These debates have also entered public discourse in relation to the highly profiled deaths of Karen Ann Quinlan, Teresa Schiavo, and Jahi McMath in the United States.[15] I suggest that a reason why brain death has been subject to such intense scholarly critique and captivated a public intoxicated with the spectacle of 'premature death' is that historically legal institutions considered "definitions of death as entirely a matter of medical judgment beyond the purview of lawmakers".[16] What changed between the invention of the iron lung in the 1930s and the development of life-supporting technologies in the 1960s, and what catapulted the problem of how law defines death onto the public stage, was that legal institutions purported to partially replace subjective medical judgment with an objective legal definition of death.[17] However, as Joshua Shaw argues, any definition remains a 'fiction' because it fails to account for "the spatio-legal features of dying", which undermine the objectivity of legal epistemologies

---

13 [1993] AC 789, 863 (Lord Goff).

14 See, for example, the collection of essays in Stuart J Youngner, Robert M Arnold and Renie Schapiro (eds), *The Definition of Death: Contemporary Controversies* (Johns Hopkins University Press, 1999) and *Defining Death: Organ Transplantation and the Fifty-Year Legacy of the Harvard Report on Brain Death*, Hastings Center Report 48, No. 6 (Hastings Center, 2018).

15 Michele Goodwin points out that Jahi McMath's death is not only "a study of brain death", but a case of "racial bias and unequal treatment, both real and perceived": Revisiting Death: Implicit Bias and the Case of Jahi McMath' in *Defining Death* (n 14) S78.

16 R Alta Charo, 'Dusk, Dawn, and Defining Death: Legal Classifications and Biological Categories' in Youngner, Arnold and Schapiro (n 14) 281.

17 For an insightful analysis of the history of scientific objectivity see, Lorraine Daston and Peter Galison, *Objectivity* (Zone Books, 2010).

in construing death "as self-evident and authoritative postulates of physicians' organic jurisprudence".[18]

Debates concerning whether brain death means the death of the whole brain or only part of it have catalysed conversations about whether death can ever be objectively determined by medical and legal institutions. In fact, there are currently calls for the definition to be changed to indicate that a person can be legally dead even where "some brain functioning continues".[19] The broader problem, though, of whether definitions of death are subjective or objective reveals the extent to which the medical profession has not handed over to legal institutions the reins for determining that a person has died. If brain death, then, is critiqued as too subjective a definition for determining whether a person has died, it is not because, as Arthur Caplan notes, it is less objective to determining death due to cardiopulmonary failure. Instead, it is because "[d]eath is a biological but also a normative concept that varies from place to place, over time, and with the introduction of new diagnostic technology".[20] What's more, any determination of death is as dependent upon a legal definition that purports to be objective, as it is on the vicissitudes of time and the contingencies of space: "It takes time, a lot of time, for every cell in our bodies to putrefy and die, and pinpointing an exact moment of death is very difficult".[21]

This section has examined how legal institutions responded to biotechnological innovations in the twentieth century that were designed to prolong, sustain, and support human life. The invention of the iron lung, modern ventilator, intensive care units, and cardiac support devices extended human life to the extent that death became an epistemological problem in law. In adopting cardiopulmonary and neurological failure as a bifurcated definition of death, legal institutions played an important role in adjudicating when a living person moves into the domain of death. They likewise occupied a central position in deciding whether it is lawful for a hospital to withdraw life-supporting technology from a near-dead patient and whether surgeons can legitimately retrieve transplantable organs from a heart-beating donor. While the medical profession monopolised these roles prior to the 1960s, the history of the codification of a definition of death reveals the extent to which medicine has preserved a role alongside law in arbitrating the threshold of when life becomes death.

---

18 Joshua David Michael Shaw, 'The Spatio-Legal Production of Bodies Through the Legal Fiction of Death' (2021) 32 *Law and Critique* 69, 72.
19 Adam Omelianchuk, et al., 'Revise the Uniform Determination of Death Act to Align the Law with Practice Through Neurorespiratory Criteria' (2022) 98 *Neurology* 532.
20 Arthur Caplan, 'Death: An Evolving, Normative Concept' in *Defining Death* (n 14) S61.
21 Ibid.

In the next section, I argue that the enactment of legal definitions of death was never simply a 'neutral' response to biotechnological innovation. It evolved from a concern with how to preserve limited resources in hospitals by withdrawing futile treatment from dying persons and how to meet an insatiable demand for organ transplantation by increasing the supply of heart-beating cadavers. To put this differently, I contend that defining the moment of death was, and still is, contingent on economic questions of resource allocation, cost-benefit calculations, and supply and demand, that at a basic register requires consideration of "the burdens on patients and families as well as on hospitals and on patients needing hospital beds occupied by comatose patients".[22] Moving beyond debates about whether definitions of death are legal fictions or social constructs, I want to explore in the next section how they have become economised in the twenty-first century.

Economising Death

Michel Foucault's lectures on 'Governmentality', delivered at the Collège de France in 1978, introduce another facet to the emergence of bio-power in the West in the eighteenth century.

> The word 'economy', which in the sixteenth century signified a form of government, comes in the eighteenth century to designate a level of reality, a field of intervention through a series of complex processes that I regard as absolutely fundamental to our history.[23]

The concept of economy was expanded from its limited designation of the activities of households to a more extensive description of the circulation of people, goods, and things in a territory. The exercise of bio-power, as I discussed in Chapter 1, entailed developing a range of political technologies for managing the vicissitudes of life and death. This notably included *thanato-politics*, which Foucault coins to emphasise how technologies for managing death, and controlling its rhythms, appeared alongside, intertwined with, and immanent to the governance of life. In 'Governmentality', however, it is unequivocal that the creation of the discipline of economics, and the positing of the economy as a problem for governmental intervention, became inextricable from bio-power and its political technologies in the eighteenth to twentieth

---

22 Robert M Veatch, 'Would a Reasonable Person Now Accept the 1968 Harvard Brain Death Report? A Short History of Brain Death' in *Defining Death* (n 14) S6. See also Martin S Pernick, 'Brain Death in a Cultural Context: The Reconstruction of Death, 1967–1981' in Youngner, Arnold and Schapiro (n 14) 3–33.

23 Michel Foucault, 'Governmentality' in Graham Burchell, Colin Gordon and Peter Miller (eds), *The Foucault Effect: Studies in Governmentality* (University of Chicago Press, 1991) 93.

centuries. Foucault explicitly reveals this entanglement in the first volume of *The History of Sexuality*, where he writes that bio-power was "an indispensable element in the development of capitalism; the latter would not have been possible without the controlled insertion of bodies into the machinery of production and the adjustment of the phenomena of population to economic processes".[24]

The dispersal of the political technologies of bio-power throughout society rather than concentrated in the figure of the sovereign is a key aspect of the development of capitalism in the nineteenth and twentieth centuries. "The adjustment of the accumulation of men to that of capital, the joining of the growth of human groups to the expansion of productive forces and the differential allocation of profit", Foucault writes, "were made possible in part by the exercise of bio-power in its many forms and modes of application".[25] What this means is that the idea that each state has an economy, and the notion that it requires governmental intervention, were not neutral propositions. They were formed in part precisely through those technologies of power, which operated at both the levels of the body and the population, to incite, control, and invest in life. The indispensable relationship between capitalism and bio-power shows how the latter was as concerned with the management of life as it was with creating the economic conditions that would foster its growth. In disseminating a discourse of 'economic rationality' throughout society, bio-power optimises life, manages its fluctuations, and governs its vagaries. It also reifies, amongst other things, as essential to a governmentality of life, the truth of economic thought.

The application of economic thought into all domains of life and death, whether that may be human activities that are already conceived of as predominantly economic, or others that may have never been thought of before through this conceptual abstraction, would be for Foucault emblematic of neoliberalism in the twentieth century.[26] Wendy Brown expands upon Foucault's writings on the figure of *homo oeconomicus*, that is, the ideal of the economically rational human being, and applies it to understand the specific arrangements of neoliberalism in the twenty-first century. Brown notes that "[w]idespread economization of heretofore noneconomic domains, activities, and subjects does not necessarily denote the marketization or monetization of them".[27]

---

24 Michel Foucault, *The History of Sexuality, Volume 1: The Will to Knowledge*, tr Robert Hurley (Penguin Books, 1998) 140–141.

25 Ibid 141.

26 Michel Foucault, *The Birth of Biopolitics: Lectures at the College de France 1978–1979*, tr Graham Burchell (Picador, 2008) 323. In these lectures, Foucault writes a comprehensive history of liberalism and neoliberalism, particularly German and American neoliberalism, in the twentieth century.

27 Wendy Brown, *Undoing the Demos: Neoliberalism's Stealth Revolution* (Zone Books, 2015) 31–32.

The difference between neoliberalism and capitalism, then, is how the former extends techniques of economisation into all spheres of life without necessarily monetising human activity. Neoliberalism is irreducible to the accumulation of capital, the creation of a free market, or the privatisation of public goods. Instead, it is a 'governing rationality' that frames and measures every aspect of life and death by "economic terms and metrics".[28] What this ultimately denotes is that a condition of possibility of contemporary life is a historically specific form of economic rationality, which extols, for example, human beings to privilege future benefits over immediate gains, transform themselves into human capital, and optimise the economic value of death.

If neoliberal rationality has become a distinctive form of governance in the twenty-first century, it is because it constructs persons and states on the model of corporate firms and self-investing, future-oriented entrepreneurs, who participate in an economy of human capital by competing against each other. Economisation is a model for the conduct of government, as well as a model for the government of the self, where persons, states, and firms transform society into a market and themselves into market actors. The *homo oeconomicus* that Foucault introduces in his lectures on bio-politics – and who, as he notes, appears in the writings of John Stuart Mill – becomes a market actor that "takes its shape [everywhere] as human capital seeking to strengthen its competitive positioning and appreciate its value, rather than as a figure of exchange or interests".[29] In *Undoing the Demos*, Brown also builds upon Koray Çaliskan and Michel Callon's performative concept of economisation to describe "behaviours, organizations, institutions and, more generally, the objects in a particular society . . . as 'economic'".[30] Brown deploys this term to account for how *homo oeconomicus* as an ideal state of being extends into areas of life that were once thought of as not exclusively or primarily economic. In the remainder of this chapter, I use this intellectual tool to understand how legal definitions of death have become subject to the governing logic of economisation in the twenty-first century.

Fatmir Haskaj's analysis of the necro-economy seeks to account for how death has become a source of economic value due to "neoliberalism's tendency to marketize all aspects of human activity".[31] Indebted

---

28   Ibid 10.
29   Ibid 33.
30   Koray Çaliskan and Michel Callon, 'Economization, Part 1: Shifting Attention from the Economy Towards Processes of Economization' (2009) 38(3) *Economy and Society* 369, 370.
31   Fatmir Haskaj, 'From Biopower to Necroeconomies: Neoliberalism, Biopower and Death Economies' (2018) 44(10) *Philosophy and Social Criticism* 1148, 1149. See also on this topic, Subhabrata Bobby Banerjee, 'Necrocapitalim' (2008) 29(12) *Organization Studies* 1541, and Patricia J Lopez and Kathryn A Gillespie (eds), *Economies of Death: Economic Logics of Killable Life and Grievable Death* (Taylor & Francis Group, 2015).

to Achille Mbembe's *Necro-politics*, Haskaj focuses on how killings due to war, genocide, poverty, starvation, and global warming create necro-economies. Yet, as I argued in Chapter 1, the problem with conceptualising death as a negative of bio-politics is that it misses how death, whether sudden or expected, unnatural or ordinary, violent or accidental, is normalised as *allowable* by the state. While I will discuss how death is normalised in Chapter 3, it will suffice for now to reiterate that the necro-economy is not exclusive of bio-power, and death is not the negation of a politics of life, because the institutional routinisation of mortality, and the political technologies that take care of those deaths, are immanent to techniques of economisation. In one sense, necro-economics could describe an arrangement of bio-power, but only if, as Warren Montag writes, death is conceived of as a condition of possibility of life – that is to say, if one examines the market and the state as entities that call for, make demands of, and allow for death in an economic rationalisation of life. In this schema of necro-economics, I suggest it is possible to frame the figure of *homo oeconomicus* as one "who with impunity may be allowed to die, slowly or quickly, in the name of the rationality and equilibrium of the market".[32]

Even though Haskaj admits that governments may abandon life under neoliberalism, the primary focus of the conceptual framework of necro-economics is to understand how governments intentionally kill populations.[33] I contend that this schema is unable to account for how individuals or segments of a population, in the course of everyday life, are *allowed* to die by the market, the state, and a panoply of institutions. Indeed, this chapter is focused on how legal institutions ordinarily allow individuals to die by defining death in economic terms. Dying *in*, rather than *for*, the economy connotes how death is always already subject to the *raison d'être* of neoliberalism, such as the replacement of exchange with competition, the substitution of individual life with human capital, and the augmentation of socio-economic inequality. In this extension of techniques of economisation into a domain that was once thought of as not exclusively or primarily economic, death circulates in an economy as valuable in itself.

---

32 Warren Montag, 'Necro-Economics: Adam Smith and Death in the Life of the Universal' (2005) 134 *Radical Philosophy* 7, 17.

33 "But the abandonment of 'life' . . . does not sufficiently cover the resonance of a global economic system that produces regimes that cannibalize their own population as vessels for a 'quantum of value'. To abandon life is simply to ignore it, or to exclude segments of the population from any share of the social product. This is certainly one tendency under neoliberalism, the tendency toward undoing of the welfare state and assault upon the poor. But exclusion alone . . . is but one side of the process that also directly and deliberately instrumentalizes human life and human death": Haskaj (n 31) 1155.

The language of economisation suffuses legal definitions of death across two registers. The first emphasises how the definition emerged from discussions by the Harvard Ad Hoc Committee, which were reiterated in numerous legal forums since then, about the necessity of rationing healthcare resources and calculating the costs and benefits of treatment in clinical settings. The second, which is more explicit than the first, concerns how economic models of supply and demand influenced legal decision-makers to create a definition of death that would increase the production of transplantable organs. Both registers can be discerned in the committee reports, law reform commissions, parliamentary debates, judicial findings and public discourse that all led to the codification of a new definition of death in the 1980s. The central argument in this chapter is that legal definitions of death have become subject to a governing logic of economisation, and it is important to recognise this to comprehend how legal institutions reify the value of death in the twenty-first century.

It is perhaps uncontroversial to point out that the Harvard Ad Hoc Committee considered, when devising a new definition of death, whether a patient in an irreversible coma uselessly consumes healthcare resources. Only seven years earlier, the renowned American economist Theodore Schultz deployed the term 'human capital' to account for how consumption can enhance human productivity, and he wrote that governments need to invest in this form of capital to grow the American economy. Expenditure on healthcare, for Schultz, which can increase "the life expectancy, strength and stamina, and the vigor and vitality of a people", and consequently improve the productivity of the American workforce, was nothing other than an investment in human capital.[34] Michael Grossman, another American economist, made this link even more explicit by coining 'health capital', and producing an economic model to understand the supply and demand for 'good health' in society. The connections that Grossman drew between markets, health, consumption, and productivity are such that death can only be conceived of quantitively as something that "occurs when the stock falls below a certain level".[35] Indeed, for Grossman, death almost appeared as a 'choice' for those individuals who do not invest in themselves as human capital. The idea, then, that a brain-dead patient may deprive others of healthcare resources, which due to their scarcity requires rationing at a local, national and global level, was simply the application of economic thought to a domain that was not previously or only indirectly considered as pertinent to the growth of the economy.

---

34 Theodore W Schultz, 'Investment in Human Capital' (1961) 51(1) *American Economic Review* 1, 9.
35 Michael Grossman, 'On the Concept of Health Capital and the Demand for Health' (1972) 80(2) *Journal of Political Economy* 223, 225.

Questions about resource allocation, scarcity, and rationing featured prominently in the deliberations of the Harvard Ad Hoc Committee in the 1960s, numerous law reform commissions throughout the 1970s, and the President's Commission on *Defining Death* in the 1980s. Discourses of economic rationality continue to circulate in the twenty-first century by economists, lawyers, clinicians, and politicians such that it is difficult not to see how the legal definition of death has become subject to a governing logic of economisation.[36] The definition of death as either cardiopulmonary or neurological failure is oriented towards making death as efficient as possible to minimise a wastage of resources, and directing limited healthcare expenditure towards optimising life. In other words, where there is a finite number of resources, competing demands for them, and their wastage is counter to economic rationality, creating a legal definition of death that will transform futility into utility will be applauded as economic good sense. Or to put it in the language of Schultz and Grossman, any way in which the process for diagnosing death can be made more efficient is a good investment in human capital. Enacting a legal definition of brain death, then, which permits clinicians to declare a person in an irreversible coma as dead, and thus lawfully withdraw technology that is keeping their bodies alive, involves making a cost-benefit calculation about the allocation and rationing of healthcare resources. While the presumption of this calculation is that a brain-dead person cannot be reanimated, and thus the use of scarce resources to support their living death is futile, the codification of brain death in law reiterates this reasoning to justify the withdrawal of treatment to allow individuals to die.

Economic rationality, however, is also a technique that can be harnessed by clinicians when they are diagnosing whether a person has legally died. The decision to maintain in the legal definition of death the proviso that only the medical profession can develop criteria for diagnosing when a person has died recognises the importance of cost-benefit calculations in a clinical setting. This section acknowledges that clinicians routinely rationalise healthcare resources, particularly in emergency departments, and they weigh up the costs and benefits of their decisions when choosing who should be given life-saving treatment and who should be allowed to die. I must point out here that these decisions are harrowing and complex, and I am not suggesting that clinicians simply disregard their Hippocratic Oath to preserve the sanctity of life, when assessing the value of saving one person's life over another. Rather I am proposing that when faced with a scarcity of resources, the decision about whether to withdraw

---

36 For an insightful analysis of debates about economic scarcity in hospice care in the United States see, Roi Livne, 'Economies of Dying: The Moralization of Economic Scarcity in U.S. Hospice Care' (2014) 79(5) *American Sociological Review* 888.

life-support technology from one person and give it to another is contingent upon discourses of economic rationality. In addition, in the clinical setting, the dying – or rather the family of the dying – must perform *homo oeconomicus*: "an intensely constructed and governed bit of human capital tasked with improving and leveraging its competitive positioning and with enhancing its (monetary and non-monetary) portfolio value across all of its endeavors and venues".[37] They are required to leverage any remnants of their human capital, adopt a competitive positioning, and commit to value seeking in order to convince the clinician to maintain the allocation of healthcare resources that are supporting their life. The point that I am making here is that the codification of brain death authorises clinicians to undertake a cost-benefit calculation to decide when a person is dead, and it asks the dying, or their families, to position themselves as *homo oeconomicus*, and thus convince the clinician, the hospital, or even a judge that the allocation of healthcare resources is an efficacious investment in the productivity of human life.

The deployment of economic rationality in medical judgments about when to switch off life-support technology, which may be specific to a particular hospital, region, or state, are supported by macro-economic discourses disseminated by medical, legal, and actuarial institutions. The *Lancet Commission on the Value of Death*, for example, which was discussed at the beginning of this book, notes that determinations of whether medical treatment is futile or useful, and whether it should be withdrawn or maintained, are made at both the level of the individual and that of the population:

> To minimise overtreatment, many governments employ cost-effectiveness thresholds, which set limits on additional funding for health gains. These thresholds are typically presented in terms of the cost per quality adjusted life year (QALY) gained.[38]

In other words, the economisation of death can be found at different levels of society, from clinicians deciding how to allocate resources in a hospital setting to governments conducting cost-benefit calculations to decide the level of their investments in healthcare resources. The proliferation of 'health-adjusted life expectancy' and 'quality adjusted life year' tables, which are created by bureaus of statistics to track mortality rates and the life expectancy of a population, inform decision-making at both the local and national levels about the economic value of death.[39]

---

37 Brown (n 27) 10.
38 'Report of the *Lancet* Commission on the Value of Death: Bringing Death Back into Life' (2022) 399 *Lancet* 837, 861.
39 In a similar vein, Katherine Kenny contends that the World Bank's DALY metric frames "health as a form of human capital and . . . as a site of *investment*". The DALY metric was invented to quantify the "global burden of disease" by calculating rates of death,

What is considered futile or valuable will depend upon who is making this decision and the perspectives of that decision-maker. However, what the legal definitions of death reveal is the extent to which economic rationality is integrated into any decision-making about when a person can be defined in law as dead and when medical treatment can be lawfully withdrawn from a brain-dead person.

The second register that demonstrates how the language of economisation suffuses legal definitions of death is more explicit in its reliance on economic thought than questions about healthcare resource allocation. This is because the economic model of supply and demand was relied upon by a range of decision-makers to justify the change in the definition for the purposes of increasing the production of transplantable organs. Faced with a shortage of supply and an increase of demand, the legal recognition of neurological failure as death was considered the most efficient way to retrieve viable organs for transplantation. Here, the near-dead patient, who may still have a beating heart, functions as a useful – not futile – vessel for organ procurement. Whereas the dying person in the first register had to present themselves as human capital, or rather the family of the brain-dead patient would have to justify the expense of keeping them alive through their connection to life-supporting technology, in the second register the definition of brain dead transforms the living cadaver into capital itself. The near-dead body becomes an object to harvest for the continuity of human life, and in an almost feedback loop with the first register, circulates in an economy that requires both the living and the dying to compete as human capital for a scarcity of healthcare resources.

Conclusion

This chapter has examined how legal definitions of death became economised in the twentieth century. The orientation towards a neurological definition of death emerged through law reform processes, where discussions about when medical treatment for persons with severe brain damage can be lawfully withdrawn were contingent on economic questions of resource allocations, cost-benefit calculations, and supply and demand. I have thus suggested that the codification of a bifurcated definition of death was, and still is, inextricable from a neoliberal rationality that has subjugated, normalised, and measured all spheres of life and death according to economic terms. It may be odd to think of decision-making about when a person has legally died and when it is lawful to withdraw life-support technology from a brain-dead patient, in relation

disease and disability together, or rather "mortality and morbidity in the same unit of analysis": Katherine E Kenny, 'The Biopolitics of Global Health: Life and Death in Neoliberal Time' (2015) 51(1) *Journal of Sociology* 9, 11. See also, Michelle Murphy, *The Economization of Life* (Duke University Press, 2017).

to notions of economisation, but as I have shown, neoliberal rationality has extended itself into domains that were once thought of as not exclusively economic since at least the beginning of the twentieth century. Individuals are fashioning themselves as *homo oeconomicus*, and they are assessing their capacity to perform human capital by reference to an economic rationality constituted as "sophisticated common sense, a reality principle remaking institutions and human beings everywhere it settles, nestles, and gains affirmation".[40]

It is important to recognise how the language of economisation suffuses relations between life and death and how techniques of resource allocation, cost-benefit calculations, and economic models of supply and demand permeate legal definitions of death. Qualitative judgments about the economic value of death underpin decision-making in medical institutions – the rationalisation of medical resources in emergency departments – and at the level of government – the development of policies and enforcement of laws that involve cost-benefit calculations about the amount of death that can be tolerated by a population. But these judgments also operate at the level of the self, and it is thus necessary to examine how legal institutions authorise economisation as a model for the government of self, which will lead to differential experiences of dying. In economising legal definitions of death, the brain-dead patient is compelled to fashion themselves as *homo oeconomicus* and they do so in a way that demonstrates how economic rationality is inextricable from the governance of death in the twenty-first century.

Further Reading

- Ad Hoc Committee of the Harvard Medical School, 'A Definition of Irreversible Coma: Report of the Ad Hoc Committee of the Harvard Medical School to Examine the Definition of Brain Death' (1968) 205(6) *Journal of the American Medical Association* 337.
- Brown, Wendy, *Undoing the Demos: Neoliberalism's Stealth Revolution* (Zone Books, 2015).
- Cantor, Norman L, *After We Die: The Life and Times of the Human Cadaver* (Georgetown University Press, 2010).
- Foucault, Michel, *The Birth of Biopolitics: Lectures at the Collège de France 1978–1979*, tr Graham Burchell (Picador, 2008).
- Lock, Margaret, *Twice Dead: Organ Transplants and the Reinvention of Death* (University of California Press, 2002).
- 'Report of the Lancet Commission on the Value of Death: Bringing Death Back into Life' (2022) 399 *Lancet* 837.

40 Brown (n 27) 35.

3

Counting the Dead

Introduction

Michel Foucault's account of the governance of plagues in the early modern period provides a cautionary tale of how power can be exercised in the time of a pandemic. The 'great confinement' of everyday life, which was designed to eradicate the plague from a town, involved closing borders, spatial partitioning, isolating infected houses, enforcing stay-at-home orders, and instituting a hierarchy of intendants, syndics, and guards, who kept watch over all movements inside and outside of the town. In contrast to the banishment of lepers in the Middle Ages, the quarantining of the sick, the fumigation of infested premises, and the confiscation of the dead after nightfall established a positive model for exercising power during the plague. Communications between different households were not simply forbidden; they were vigorously surveilled when a family member left their house once a week to purchase essential goods. Techniques of observation relied upon acts of permanent registration, or rather, the extent to which power was exercised effectively, depended on practices for recording the visual examinations of intendants, syndics, and guards, and enumerating the recent dead in bills of mortality. The plague was a "marvellous moment" of disciplinary power, Foucault writes in *Abnormal*; it was a "political dream of an exhaustive, unobstructed power that is completely transparent to its object and exercised to the full".[1]

The continuities between the governance of plagues in the sixteenth to eighteenth centuries, and the administrative management of a pandemic in the twenty-first century, are uncanny. The public health response to the COVID-19 pandemic initially involved in 2020 extensive interventions into everyday life, such as curfews, lockdowns, border closures, ring fencing, quarantine orders, mandatory testing, and other

1 Michel Foucault, *Abnormal: Lectures at the Collège de France, 1974–1975*, tr Graham Burchell (Picador, 2003) 47.

DOI: 10.4324/9781003222163-3

social distancing restrictions, which – akin to the legislative measures instituted in plague towns – maximised the vitality of populations, while also *allowing* people to die. The rationalisation of medical resources – articulated first by emergency doctors in hospitals in Italy during the first wave of SARS-CoV-2, the virus that causes COVID-19, and then by 'death panels' hastily set up in the United States – were nothing new for medical institutions in the twenty-first century but revealed, perhaps too honestly, the extent to which governments will calculate the social, political, and economic costs of "*foster*[ing] life or *disallow*[ing] it to the point of death".[2] The pandemic confirmed, much like the epidemics that preceded it, that even if "death is power's limit, the moment that escapes it", as Foucault emphasises in the first volume of *The History of Sexuality*, governments have never ceased attempting to control death.[3]

Yet this model of the plague is not the endpoint of the tale that Foucault narrates of how power can be exercised in the time of a pandemic. In *Security, Territory, Population*, a lecture series at the Collège de France that followed *Abnormal* by a couple of years, Foucault extrapolates from his description of the management of plagues, singling out the smallpox epidemics that ravaged much of the world during the eighteenth and nineteenth centuries. The notable difference with smallpox was the widespread distribution of a vaccine by the end of the nineteenth century and the eradication of the disease in the mid-twentieth century. Foucault describes the emergence of vaccination regimes as transformative in how communicable diseases could be managed by governments. Vaccination became an apparatus of securitisation of a population – indeed, a population, as opposed to a city or town, became a target of administrative intervention – but one that was conceptualised according to a "calculus of probabilities".[4]

The disciplinary powers developed in the governance of plagues in the early modern period did not disappear with public health responses to the epidemics and pandemics that inundated the world in the nineteenth to twenty-first centuries. However, what appeared in the administration of vaccination, initially developed to combat the scourge of smallpox (*la petite vérole*) in the late eighteenth century, was the concept of a population that could be studied as a scientific object. In this arrangement of governmentality, a population was made sense of through the development of secular death registration procedures, classification systems for death causation, statistical tabulations of mortality rates, and

---

2   Michel Foucault, *The History of Sexuality, Volume 1: The Will to Knowledge*, tr Robert Hurley (Penguin Books, 1998) 138 (emphasis in original).
3   Ibid.
4   Michel Foucault, *Security, Territory, Population: Lectures at the Collège de France, 1977–1978*, tr Graham Burchell (Palgrave Macmillan, 2004) 59.

calculations of probabilities of life expectancy. These technologies were vital for how public health reformers determined what causes of death should be monitored at different levels of the population. They cohered in creating the idea, first cemented in the eighteenth century, but enduring to this very day, that every population has a 'normal' rate of death.

This chapter examines how death is registered during a pandemic and how each registration becomes enumerated in a statistical tabulation of mortality rates. Whereas the previous chapter explored how legal definitions of death have become subject to the governing logic of economisation, this chapter investigates how laws of registration recognise statistical value in death. Technologies of registration depend on the creation of universal nomenclature for ascertaining death causation, which excludes various circumstances of a life to stabilise a communicable disease as a normative category for classification. This means that the registration of a death is conditioned upon differentiating between the normal and the pathological, standards and variations, and an average and excess. The point that I will make in this chapter is not that registration as a normalising technology is problematic in itself – classification systems cannot operate without norms – but rather how the technology can be harnessed during a pandemic to pathologise specific kinds of death while unproblematically reifying the concept of a normal death. In what follows, I will argue that laws of registration are intertwined with political technologies for managing a population and that pandemics expose the role they perform in constructing a 'natural' state of the population. Registration is a normalising technology that is inextricable from how state institutions determine what deaths count.

Death Registration

The transformation from clerical to secular death registration in the eighteenth century in France, and the nineteenth century in Germany and Britain, anticipated the popularisation of public health in the late nineteenth century. The French Republic commenced the civil registration of all deaths in a municipality in the late eighteenth century, where previously only burials were recorded by the Church. The enactment of the *Births and Deaths Registration Act 1836* (UK), which established a General Register Office in England and Wales and vested a public servant, the Registrar-General, with the responsibility of registering every death in a geographical area, likewise removed the duty of recording all burials in a parish from religious institutions. The administrative regime of mortality record-keeping relied upon the mapping of discrete 'registration' districts, a hierarchy of supervisors and delegates, and a legion of coroners and physicians, who signed death certificates, setting out the age, sex, and rank of the deceased, as well as the ostensible cause of death. For Thomas Laqueur and Lisa Cody, "[a]ll over Europe the dead entered the administrative world of trash, water, and other waste. They entered the domain of new experts on what to do with matter".[5] Public health reformers in Britain, particularly Edwin Chadwick, William Farr, and John Snow, brandished civil death registration as a turning point for improving the sanitary conditions of a 'labouring' population, and alongside other legislative reforms in the nineteenth century, it paved the way for the development of the science of epidemiology.

In the *History of Sexuality*, Foucault refers to death registration as part of a suite of institutional practices that correlate with the emergence of bio-power in the West. The practices of registering a death, classifying its cause, arranging it in a table, and calculating its probabilities all constitute different technologies of *thanato-politics*, which as I mentioned in the introduction to this book was a term coined by Foucault to emphasise that *bio-politics* does not ignore death. In fact, the manifestation of death as an 'insurmountable' limit of power's control over life renders visible how a range of state and non-state institutions attempt to manage what always already slips outside of their grasp. Foucault makes this point clear in *Society Must be Defended*: "[d]eath is beyond the reach of power, and power has a grip on it only in general, overall, or statistical terms".[6] Bio-power as a new 'art of government' concerned itself not simply with the management of a population in a general sense but offered precise points of intervention, at different levels of the population, for the purposes of monitoring, and even manipulating, fluctuations in economies of death. If the government of a population in the exercise of bio-power involves the practice of 'taking care' of things and their relations, then the quantification of those relations, not only their qualitative value, become 'technical vectors' of governmentality.

It is no coincidence that mortality statistics gained popularity around the same time that death became an object of registration. Statistics first emerged as a technology for organising knowledge of the state in the seventeenth century, but by the nineteenth century, governments were drowning in an inundation of numbers – the enumeration of illness, households, welfare, taxes, suicides, and crime – that revealed a regularity to life. Ian Hacking writes of statistics as the "taming of chance",[7] a set of rules or norms for governing probabilities of phenomena. He presents mortality statistics as a definitive example of the erosion of determinism

---

5 Thomas Laqueur and Lisa Cody, 'Birth and Death Under the Sign of Thomas Malthus' in Michael Sappol and Stephen P Rice (eds), *A Cultural History of the Human Body: In the Age of Empire: Volume 5* (Berg, 2010) 41.

6 Michel Foucault, *Society Must Be Defended: Lectures at the Collège de France, 1975–1976*, tr David Macey (Picador, 2003) 248.

7 Ian Hacking, *The Taming of Chance* (Cambridge University Press, 1990).

and the organisation of chance according to classification systems. John Graunt, who published *Natural and Political Observations Mentioned in a Following Index, and made upon the Bills of Mortality* in 1662, pioneered the art of statistical analysis. He collated weekly counts of the dead in London and categorised them according to cause, age, and sex in order to identify mortality trends. He was the first to "show that death is not governed by random strokes of fate but rather by stable and quantifiable patterns".[8] However much Graunt insisted that his analyses were objective descriptions of the reality of death, the substitution of a quantifiable fact for the caprices of fate exposed the extent to which he actively constructed this reality. Early statistical laws of mortality were rudimentary, but they classified death causation according to a set of agreed probabilities that could be enumerated in a table. Despite the difficulties of ascertaining every cause of death, for Graunt and others in the seventeenth century, "to die of anything except causes on the official list . . . [was] illegal, for example, to die of old age".[9]

While Graunt, who was a haberdasher, pursued statistical analysis as a pastime, and his writings were routinely ignored by governments, by the late nineteenth century mortality statistics became indispensable tools for determining the wealth, health, and strength of populations. Not only were statistics fastidiously collated through death registration systems, but also legions of statisticians were employed by governments to interpret and make sense of the oscillating rhythms of life and death. The diverse range of 'official lists' that circulated throughout the West in the seventeenth century were superseded in the nineteenth century by universal nomenclature, authored by physician turned statistician Jacques Bertillon and appropriately titled the *Bertillon Classification of Causes of Death*. The lawfulness of death registration, which depended on a commonly defined classification system, became of immense value for state and non-state institutions, and particularly for the newly disciplines of public health, epidemiology, and demography. Statistical analyses of records of death were harnessed by a panoply of institutions to define the shape of a population, monitor its variations and fluctuations,

---

8 Zohreh Bayatrizi, 'Counting the Dead and Regulating the Living: Early Modern Statistics and the Formation of the Sociological Imagination (1662–1897)' (2009) 60(3) *British Journal of Sociology* 603, 612. See also, Zohreh Bayatrizi, *Life Sentences: The Modern Ordering of Mortality* (University of Toronto Press, 2008).

9 Ian Hacking, 'How Should We Do the History of Statistics?' in Graham Burcell, Colin Gordon and Peter Miller (eds), *The Foucault Effect: Studies in Governmentality* (University of Chicago Press, 1991) 183. Hacking has updated this quote for contemporary times by noting "[i]t is illegal to die, nowadays, of any cause except those prescribed in a long list drawn up by the World Health Organization (WHO)": Ian Hacking, 'Biopower and the Avalanche of Printed Numbers' in Vernon W Cisney and Nicolae Morar (eds), *Biopower: Foucault and Beyond* (University of Chicago Press, 2016) 66.

predict patterns of dying, highlight risk factors, and ultimately intervene in the conditions of life to manipulate the 'average' life expectancy of a population.

The secularisation of death registration in the nineteenth century was thus integral to statistical laws of mortality because it made possible the institutional practice of extrapolating death from an individual life and arranging it in a table in an enumerated form. Registration drained death of all its phenomena, abstracted it as a number, and weaved its laws into the seams of a population. In ascertaining the cause of a death and monitoring trends in mortality at different levels of a population over a specific duration, governments could construct its 'natural' state. Statisticians could tame the chance of death, that is, calculate the risk of death in a population, for instance, that could be derived from a pandemic, and according to the science of epidemiology attempt to "change the laws under which the population would evolve".[10] Populations have long lived under elaborate laws of classification, Hacking reminds us, such as the laws of death registration and classification systems for death causation, which both shape a calculus of probabilities of dying. The registration of a death by state institutions and its quantification as a rate that can be measured was indispensable to how governments in the nineteenth and twentieth centuries invested in life to the point where individuals were *allowed* to die.

Death registration systems remain ubiquitous across much of the world in the twenty-first century. Most jurisdictions have an integrated system for permanently recording a death, even though participation in the bureaucratic process that imprints the dead in the register can be burdensome, inequitable, and Kafkaesque. Registration procedures provide the living with access to legal, medical, social, and financial services in the wake of a death while also offering governments tools for managing the dynamics of a population. Modern death registration is underpinned by three institutional practices: the bureaucratic logic of the file, classification systems for death causation, and the statistical tabulation of mortality rates. The reliance on technical, written record-keeping in the nineteenth century bureaucratised earlier forms of parochial registration and transformed individual deaths into files that could be collated by state institutions. Cornelia Vismann examines the act of filing as inextricable from the formalisation of law in the West, and I have discussed elsewhere the significance of record-keeping for how legal institutions took care of the dead in the nineteenth and twentieth centuries.[11]

---

10 Ibid 188.
11 See Cornelia Vismann, *Files: Law and Media Technology*, tr Geoffrey Winthrop-Young (Stanford University Press, 2008) and Marc Trabsky, *Law and the Dead: Technology, Relations and Institutions* (Routledge, 2019) Ch 4.

The fact that state institutions transform a dead person into a file and physically or digitally store that file in a central register may no longer be surprising, even though this was a radical innovation for the governance of death in the modern era.

Classification systems for death causation, on the other hand, which keep on expanding with developments in the disciplines of nosology, pathology, epidemiology, and public health, continue to rouse debate, particularly during a global pandemic. While a lack of universal nomenclature for death causation initially persisted in the nineteenth century, a point highlighted by William Farr, the first Superintendent of Statistics at the General Registers Office in England and Wales, the pursuit of objectivity for classifying death, first proposed by Florence Nightingale and later developed by Bertillon, shaped the register as not simply a record of who died but a source of data for tracking mortality trends at different levels of the population. The register became a treasure trove for the taming of chance by the end of the nineteenth century and it remains as such in the twenty-first century. The tabulation of mortality rates, or to put this differently, the arrangement of the number of deaths per year, and across different attributes, such as age, sex, location, and cause of death, in the form of tables, conditions the possibility of the quantification of death in terms of *amounts*. In the late nineteenth century, and perhaps for the first time, the amount of death in a population in any given year became a diagnostic tool for *pathologising* variations and fluctuations in the purported rate over a specific duration. What a global pandemic exposes, then, is just how obsessed governments can be with managing knowledge of what constitutes a normal and pathological amount of death in any given population.

Normalising Death

In *The Normal and the Pathological*, Georges Canguilhem writes a history of the relationship between the concepts of the normal and the pathological in the disciplines of biology, medicine, and nosology. In the writings of Auguste Comte, François-Joseph-Victor Broussais and Claude Bernard, pathology manifests as a 'quantitative variation' (too much or too little) of a normal state of existence, while "the scientific study of pathological cases becomes an indispensable phase in the overall search for the laws of the normal state".[12] In the second part of the book, Canguilhem reiterates that the constitutive relationship between the normal and the pathological is shaped by quantitative, statistical, and mathematical concepts. The normal is "the average or standard of

---

12 Georges Canguilhem, *The Normal and the Pathological*, tr Carolyn R Fawcett and Robert S Cohen (Zone Books, 1991) 51.

a measurable characteristic", such that the pathological can only make sense as a quantifiable deviation from a norm.[13] Here, life only becomes a norm given the habitual regularity of the effectiveness of the human body, and it remains in that fragile state until the body is disrupted by disease, illness, or death.

When applying this theory to the science of biology, it becomes unequivocal that life is the normative state of the human body, and death is nothing other than an inclined variation from the functional order of things. In other words, death is not an anomaly in itself, but rather it manifests as anomalous due to its divergence in degree from the standardisation of a physiological operation. Anomaly derives from the Greek *anomalia*, which according to Canguilhem, "means unevenness, asperity; *omalos* in Greek means that which is level, even, smooth, hence 'anomaly' is, etymologically, *an-omalos*, that which is uneven, rough, irregular, in the sense given these words when speaking of a terrain".[14] Canguilhem points this out to show that anomaly does not derive etymologically from the Greek word for law, *nomos*. On the other hand, the etymology of the word abnormal lies in the nineteenth-century reshaping of the French *anormal*, which denotes non-conformity to a rule or contrary to law. Canguilhem contends that while 'anomaly' was once used as a descriptive term, and 'abnormal' was originally conceptualised as evaluative, over time the meanings of both words combined to equally refer to the making of a qualitative judgment. In depicting death as anomalous or abnormal, one is not only designating it as a matter of a fact but also offering an evaluation of that fact.

Since 2020 epidemiologists, journalists, politicians, and the public have repeatedly questioned the 'true' death toll of the COVID-19 pandemic. If the history of pandemics has taught us anything though about the difficulties of counting the dead, the question of how many people will have ultimately died from or with SARS-CoV-2 will continue to mystify the world for decades to come. It should come as no surprise that historians continue to debate the number of individuals who succumbed to the Black Death in the Late Middle Ages, the cholera pandemics in the nineteenth century, and the Spanish Flu in the twentieth century. With COVID-19, however, experts and commentators alike have argued, almost contemporaneously, that official state-based deaths tolls have been gravely inaccurate, because they either underestimated the deadliness of the pandemic or the overall mortality rates for all deaths were lower on average than previous years due to social distancing restrictions.

No matter how the mortality rate may have been calculated or miscalculated by state institutions, as Stefania Milan points out, "the

13 Ibid 125.
14 Ibid 131.

COVID-19 crisis . . . installed quantification at the core of the governmental and popular response to the virus".[15] Or as Bernard-Henri Lévy writes of the representation of COVID-19 in France, "[n]ever had a physician been invited into our households every evening to toll, like a sad Pythius, the number of the day's dead".[16] The pandemic established administrative practices of 'counting the dead' as the only way to *know* the virus that causes COVID-19, and in society's feverish propensity to enumerate mortality, death was characterised as both normal and pathological. Death-counting, whether commissioned by states, embraced by epidemiologists, questioned by politicians or critiqued by journalists, represented fatalities directly caused by the virus as anomalous, while deaths directly, indirectly, or even tangentially related to the pandemic – for example, deaths due to suicides, accidents, violence, negligence, chronic illness, or other diseases – as the inevitable resolution of a life lived well or a normal, albeit tragic, end of a life cut short.

The problem of how death appeared as both normal and pathological in the COVID-19 pandemic was contingent upon the institutional practices that underpin modern death registration: classification systems for death causation and the statistical tabulation of mortality rates. The first practice derives from how a cause of death is identified by state institutions for the purposes of registering a death. Legal procedures for completing a 'cause of death form' attribute responsibility to medical practitioners and empowers them to use medical knowledge to differentiate between underlying, associated, and multiple causes of death. 'Underlying' refers to the leading cause of death, that is, a disease or injury that 'initiated' the journey towards death, whereas 'associated' denotes an immediate, antecedent, direct, indirect, or intervening contribution to death other than the underlying cause. The reference to multiple causes signifies a combination of underlying and associated causes of a death. Practitioners responsible for signing a death certificate are obliged to indicate the cause that led directly to the death, but also any associated causes, if the underlying cause arose due to another disease, injury or condition.

The second practice, the tabulation of death rates, is dependent on how a cause of death is classified by institutions that are responsible for death registration. What was included or excluded in official state-based COVID-19 death tolls relied upon a series of administrative decisions to either only count deaths where the SARS-CoV-2 virus was identified as the underlying cause, or *also* count deaths that had a different underlying

15 Stefania Milan, 'Techno-Solutionism and the Standard Human in the Making of the COVID-19 Pandemic' (2020) *Big Data & Society* 1, 1.
16 Bernard-Henri Lévy, *The Virus in the Age of Madness* (Yale University Press, 2020) 3.

cause, but where the virus contributed to the death.[17] In the United States, for example, some states initially only reported the deaths of confirmed cases of COVID-19 to the Centers for Disease Control and Prevention (CDC) via the National Vital Statistics System and the National Center for Health Statistics, while other states reported the deaths of both confirmed and probable cases of the virus.[18] Relatively few countries reported the deaths of *suspected* cases of COVID-19, where a person met both the clinical and epidemiological criteria of the virus but did not receive a positive outcome from a relevant test prior to their death.

The complexities of the classificatory process for determining a cause of death should not be underestimated. Whether a death was counted in COVID-19 mortality statistics in 2020 and 2021 was contingent upon medical practitioners distinguishing between dying *from* the virus, where it was the direct cause of death, as opposed to dying *with* the virus, where it contributed to the death – which several epidemiologists expressed in terms of degrees and percentages – but was not the underlying cause. Yet to determine whether a person either died from or with COVID-19, medical practitioners had to first ascertain 'measurable' characteristics of each death – such as the age and sex of the deceased, the location and time of the death, any pre-existing comorbidities and whether the person tested positive for the virus prior to their death – and second, compare those characteristics against broader mortality trends. In other words, practitioners had to contrast the individual against a typical death for a specific segment of the population. This was undoubtedly gleaned from a practitioner's experience, training, and knowledge but also from their interpretation of universal nomenclature for the classification of diseases and illnesses, which since its invention in the late nineteenth century has categorised morbidities in relation to concepts of the normal and the pathological.[19]

17 In 2020, a COVID-19 death in Australia was "defined for surveillance purposes as a death in a probable or confirmed COVID-19 case, unless there is a clear alternative cause of death that cannot be related to COVID-19 (e.g., trauma). There should be no period of complete recovery from COVID-19 between illness and death": Communicable Diseases Network Australia, *Coronavirus Disease 2019 (COVID-19) CDNA National Guidelines for Public Health Units* (Version 3.8, 23 August 2020) 24.

18 See Allan Smith, 'How many died? Different ways of counting make the COVID-19 tally elusive', *NBC News*, 16 June 2020 <www.nbcnews.com/politics/politics-news/covid-19-death-tally-different-ways-counting-make-number-elusive-n1216801>. While the distinction between a probable and confirmed case was not uniform across the world, generally a confirmed case required a positive outcome from a SARS-CoV-2 nucleic acid test, PCR test or antibody test, while a probable case needed a positive outcome from an antibody test, a compatible clinical illness and met an epidemiological criteria, of a suspected case, which ranged from international travel or the person being a close contact of a confirmed or probable case in the 14 days prior to the onset of symptoms.

19 World Health Organization, *International Statistical Classification of Diseases and Related Health Problems* (ICD-10) (WHO, 10th Revision, 2018) code U07.1. This code was inserted into the tenth version of the ICD in light of the COVID-19 pandemic.

Canguilhem defines the norm as "that which conforms to the rule, regular" and "that which is met with in the majority of cases of a determined kind".[20] It etymologically derives from the Latin word *noma*, which denotes a T-square in mathematics. If Canguilhem appears to be befuddled by the meaning of this word, it is not for a want of trying to ascertain its significance. The norm is both a fact and an ideal, an objective reality and an illusory construction, and a quantitative change and a qualitative judgment. It only acquires its meaning in a dynamic relationship between the normal and the pathological (or the abnormal), and the latter constitutes everything that finds itself outside of the norm, though Canguilhem emphasises that this should not result in "a relativity of health and disease so confusing that one does not know where health ends and disease begins".[21] To normalise in biology, medicine or nosology is a process of establishing a norm of health, and this involves imposing a condition of existence on phenomena that lies outside of itself but according to rules inherent in the norm. To put this differently, to normalise is to unify disparity between health and disease, and life and death, and however much it is ultimately bound to fail, it involves for the disciplines of biology, medicine, and nosology, the taming of the dynamics of chance.

Counting the dead during COVID-19, which relied upon technologies of death registration, classification systems for death causation, and the tabulation of mortality rates, involved normalising the pathological and pathologising the normal. While a death that occurred during the pandemic may not have been counted in an official state-based COVID-19 death toll for a variety of reasons – the virus was classified as an associated, not underlying cause of death, or a laboratory test for the virus was not undertaken while the person was alive, or the person's symptoms prior to death did not meet clinical or epidemiological criteria – what is most interesting is how counting normalised specific deaths as abnormal and pathologised other deaths as inevitable. This was most apparent when considering how the privileging of a COVID-19 death toll – the creation of a new table for measuring the rate of death in a population for a particular virus – represented deaths directly caused by the virus as anomalous, while it depicted other deaths caused by the pandemic but not the virus itself, such as deaths caused by delays in planned surgeries or medical examinations, or even deaths caused directly by the influenza virus circulating the globe during the same period, as normal. Yet, and this is where the paradox explicitly manifests, a normal death during the pandemic only made sense if it corresponded to an 'average', which could be ascertained by examining mortality trends over a specified duration. So, if a death 'exceeds' that average, or when the amount

20 Canguilhem (n 12) 125.
21 Ibid 182.

of death in any given period deviates from standard rates over a specified duration, then the normal becomes pathological.

Excess Mortality

The epidemiological concept of 'excess mortality' became the subject of much fascination during the first year of the COVID-19 pandemic. The term denotes the idea that a population has a normal death rate, and it presumes as a matter of *fact* that death is an inevitable, necessary, and (perhaps for governments) a desirous outcome of life. In 2020 and 2021, excess mortality was used to describe official state-based tolls as inadequate, and it suggested that more people were dying from or with COVID-19 than had been counted by state institutions. But it was also deployed to contend that governmental responses to the pandemic caused a disproportionate amount of death that may not be counted in state-based tolls, or even narrativised or commemorated by government officials, such as deaths from eschewing urgent medical care or necessary health checks, reductions in screening, diagnosing and treating a range of diseases, illnesses and conditions, and spatial barriers to accessing time-sensitive medical treatment.[22] This was in addition to claims that an increase in deaths where the direct cause is a suicide, accident, violence, or negligence will only be discovered many years after the pandemic. Thus epidemiologists, journalists, and researchers asserted that excess mortality was a "better way of measuring the true impact of the pandemic".[23]

22 Researchers began analysing the effects of public health responses to the pandemic on time-sensitive care provided in emergency departments for cardiac and stroke conditions; barriers to screening, diagnosing, and treating cancers; postponement of elective surgery; and increases in post-operational complications due to the general avoidance of medical treatment and care as early as 2020. This was also juxtaposed by research on a lower-than-average death rate in specific jurisdictions in 2020 and 2021 due to vaccination uptake, mandatory testing regimes, mask use and handwashing, and improved infection control protocols in hospitals and aged care homes, which resulted in fewer deaths from influenza, pneumonia, motor accidents, and workplace accidents compared to the same time period in previous years. See, eg, in Australia, Dana McCauley, 'Aged care deaths fall during pandemic with influenza at record levels', *Sydney Morning Herald*, 12 September 2020 <www.smh.com.au/politics/federal/aged-care-deaths-fall-during-pandemic-with-influenza-at-record-lows-20200912-p55uzt.html>.

23 Casey Briggs, 'Coronavirus deaths could be much higher than official toll due to number of "excess deaths"', *ABC News*, 30 April 2020 <www.abc.net.au/news/2020-04-30/coronavirus-deaths-likely-higher-due-to-excess-deaths/12200850>. See also, 'Tracking covid-19 excess deaths across countries', *Economist*, 15 July 2020 <www.economist.com/graphic-detail/2020/07/15/tracking-covid-19-excess-deaths-across-countries> and 'The covid-19 pandemic is worse than official figures show',

If mortality can be described as excessive, as Canguilhem notes with regards to life tables, it is only insofar as the amount of death deviates from an average. Referring to Maurice Halbwachs, Canguilhem surmises that

[e]verything happens as if a society had 'the mortality that suits it', the number of the dead and their distribution into different age groups expressing the importance which the society does or does not give to the protraction of life [53, 95–97]. In short, the techniques of collective hygiene which tend to prolong human life, or the habits of negligence which result in shortening it, depending on the value attached to life in a given society, are in the end a value judgement expressed in the abstract number which is the average human life span. The average life span is not the biologically normal, but in a sense the socially normative, life span. Once more the norm is not deduced from, but rather expressed in the average.[24]

In other words, the measurement of excess death is made possible by its comparison to a numerical average, which is also the articulation of a qualitative judgment about the value of human life. The concept of the average, for François Ewald, is the expression of a process of normalisation that has as its aim a general consensus of what is "adequate to the purpose it was meant to serve".[25] The average is not a stable concept for it is continually changing in a cascade of comparisons. It is "a form of compromise, the common denominator, a point of reference that is destined to disappear – a measurement that expresses the relation of a group to itself, even that of a group as large as the entire population of the globe".[26] What this means is that an *average* mortality rate is not a reference to some kind of objective reality no matter how many journalists, politicians, and epidemiologists plead with the public to accept science as an unmistakeable 'voice of truth'. Rather it is the expression of a process of normalisation that can only ever refer to a multiplicity of other norms. In this schema of a 'normative order' of death, *excess* mortality is the outcome of a process that invites state institutions to register a death, monitor mortality rates, and importantly assign value to a particular kind of death in relation to another. "[T]he norm invites each one of us", Ewald writes "to imagine ourselves as different from the others,

---

Economist, 26 September 2020 <www.economist.com/briefing/2020/09/26/the-covid-19-pandemic-is-worse-than-official-figures-show>.

24   Canguilhem (n 12) 51.

25   François Ewald, 'Norms, Discipline, and the Law' (tr Marjorie Beale) (1990) 30 *Representations* 138, 152.

26   Ibid.

forcing the individual to turn back upon his or her own particular case, his or her individuality and irreducible particularity".[27]

It is for such reasons that certifying the death toll of a pandemic and employing the epidemiological concept of excess mortality to ascertain its purported truth will remain an insurmountable assignment. In the search for objectivity, statisticians labour under the Sisyphean task of distinguishing between an average and excess, standards and variations, and the normal and the pathological. It could be said though that certitude should not be the *raison d'être* for counting the dead, and the idea of excess mortality provides statisticians with the latitude to calculate an approximation of the number of individuals that may have died from or with COVID-19. To put this differently, the aim of critiquing the way in which state institutions underestimate who has died in a pandemic does not necessary result in the desire to uncover a 'true' death toll. Indeed, journalists, politicians, and epidemiologists have harnessed the prerogative rhetoric of excess to draw attention to the lives lost to the virus that remain unaccountable. This is certainly the case for vulnerable, disadvantaged, and minority communities around the world, and particularly in low-income countries, which have been disproportionately affected by COVID-19 and whose deaths are forgotten, neglected, undervalued, and incalculable.

The point that I am attempting to make here is not that the mathematics of counting the dead is true or false. Nor am I suggesting that it is disingenuous to deploy the rhetoric of excess mortality to enumerate the forgotten dead, particularly marginalised individuals who remain unaccountable in state-based death tolls. Instead, I am drawing attention to how the bureaucratic practices of counting the dead depend on qualitative determinations that not all deaths are equal. The way in which state institutions count depends on the laws of registration, which operate by normalising a death in comparison to other norms. Registration is contingent upon the creation of a universal nomenclature for ascertaining causation, which excludes various circumstances of an individual's life in order to stabilise a communicable disease as a normative category for classification. Excess mortality does not critique these practices, and instead unproblematically normalises the idea that every population has a normal amount of death, and any deviation from that norm is pathological.

The concept of excess mortality shows how the bureaucratic decision to count a death during a pandemic in an official state-based toll will depend as much on the capacity of institutions to register a death and determine its cause, as on the making of a normative judgment about what kind of deaths should be counted at all. The technology of registration makes use of classification systems for death causation and the statistical tabulation of death rates to normalise death as both an anomaly

27 Ibid 154.

and an inevitability. For every individual that dies during the COVID-19 pandemic, the registration of their death, their extraction as data in mortality tables, and the measurement of their individual death against an average enables governments to make sense of the pathological as a normal end point of a life.

In *Security, Territory, Population*, Foucault explains that the emergence of the smallpox epidemics in the eighteenth and nineteenth centuries coalesced with the problematisation of a range of probable phenomena that went unremarked in previous centuries. Governments were no longer faced with simply the questions of whether to exclude lepers or quarantine plague victims, but rather they needed to contend with innumerable questions of how to manage a population:

> how many people are infected with smallpox, at what age, with what effects, with what mortality rate, lesions or after-effects, the risks of inoculation, the probability of an individual dying or being infected by smallpox despite inoculation, and the statistical effects on the population in general.[28]

The invention of vaccination regimes across multiple segments of the population undoubtedly transformed smallpox from an uncontrollable epidemic to a manageable endemic by the early twentieth century. Foucault describes the technology of vaccination as a 'calculus of probabilities' and an 'apparatus of security' that "establishes an average considered as optimal on the one hand, and, on the other, a bandwidth of the acceptable that must not be exceeded".[29] But alongside this apparatus lay the technologies of death registration, classification systems for death causation, and the statistical tabulation of mortality rates that initially normalised smallpox deaths as pathological, and then later as part of a normal death rate of a given population.

COVID-19's journey from a pandemic to an endemic virus has been similar, albeit much swifter to that of smallpox in the twentieth century. The categorisation of a COVID-19 death as an anomaly in media outlets and government briefings in 2020, well before COVID-19 became endemic, depicted the virus as an incongruous disruption in the habitual economy of life and death. In fact, COVID-19 deaths were represented as pathological, and differed from other causes of death, particularly through their quotidian announcement in official state-based tolls. Yet the implementation of vaccination regimes from 2021 sought to normalise COVID-19 deaths as an acceptable, if not inevitable, outcome of a life for specific segments of a population. To this extent, to die

---

28 Foucault (n 4) 10.
29 Ibid 6.

of COVID-19 became comparable to those 'routine' deaths caused by the influenza virus each year. What is more though, even 'excess mortality' was normalised, particularly by the World Health Organization, which estimated in 2022 that approximately 15 million people had died during the global pandemic. The international organisation included in a worldwide toll for the first time those "killed directly or *indirectly*" by the pandemic, such as deaths caused by barriers to screening, diagnosing, and treating other medical conditions, the overwhelming of health services, or individuals avoiding or failing to receive healthcare.[30] COVID-19 deaths then, like deaths caused by smallpox or influenza, became "no longer something that suddenly swooped down on life – as in an epidemic. Death was now something permanent, something that slips into life, perpetually gnaws at it, diminishes it and weakens it".[31]

Conclusion

The history of the technology of death registration in the eighteenth and nineteenth centuries reveals how classification systems for death causation and the statistical tabulation of mortality rates occupied a vital role in the emergence of an era of bio-power, where the problem of life and death became more conspicuous in arrangements of governmentality. The COVID-19 pandemic exposes how these technologies continue to play important functions in collating, monitoring, and manipulating patterns of death in different segments of the population. It also shows how the institutional practices of recording the death of an individual in a file, abstracting it as a numerical value, and arranging amounts of death in a table are inextricable from how governments construct a 'natural' state of the population. The epistemological question of how to ascertain a 'true' death toll thus emerges in the time of a pandemic not because of an institutional appetite for suppressing the collection of mortality statistics – though this certainly may still be the case in a number of countries – but rather due to technologies for registering a death, classifying the causes of those deaths, and determining whether they deviate from an 'average', which is isomorphic from a normative judgment of how much mortality suits any given population.

30 Nicola Davis, 'WHO estimates 15m people killed directly or indirectly by Covid pandemic', *Guardian*, 6 May 2022 <www.theguardian.com/world/2022/may/05/who-estimates-15m-people-were-killed-by-covid-or-overwhelmed-health-systems> (my emphasis). "Most of the excess deaths (84%) are concentrated in South-East Asia, Europe, and the Americas": World Health Organization, '14.9 million excess deaths associated with the COVID-19 pandemic in 2020 and 2021', 5 May 2022 <www.who.int/news/item/05-05-2022-14.9-million-excess-deaths-were-associated-with-the-covid-19-pandemic-in-2020-and-2021>.
31 Foucault (n 6) 244.

This chapter has shown how the laws of death registration can be harnessed to pathologise specific kinds of death while unproblematically reifying the concept of a normal death. It has argued that legal technologies are utilised to construct a 'natural' state of the population. While perhaps unremarkable at the best of times, the COVID-19 pandemic renders visible how technical, scientific, and bureaucratic practices self-referentially conceive of death with respect to norms immanent in the population itself, norms that are the fruits of a process of normalisation that does not refer to some externally constructed truth. The normative order of classification systems for death causation and the statistical tabulation of mortality rates draw attention to how governments remain intensely invested in creating a normal rate of death for a population. Indeed, the transformation from sovereign power to bio-power in the eighteenth century did not only generate technologies that seek to incite, control, optimise, and invest life. Governmentality, as a technology of power that optimises life, has never shied away from fostering life to the point where individuals are allowed to die.

What the pandemic ultimately demonstrates is that death is as much a normal as it is a pathological outcome of a life, and a panoply of institutions quantitatively and qualitatively determine what is typical in contrast to the exceptional, and thus whether all deaths, or only certain ones, should be recorded, counted, and valued in official state-based tolls. These infinitesimal bureaucratic decisions, made by different institutions throughout society, depend on an array of administrative practices for registering a death, classifying its cause, tabulating it as a rate, and monitoring its trends, which all involve evaluative judgments about what amount of death is normal for any given population.

Further Reading

- Bayatrizi, Zohreh, *Life Sentences: The Modern Ordering of Mortality* (University of Toronto, 2008).
- Canguilhem, Georges, *The Normal and the Pathological*, tr Carolyn R Fawcett and Robert S Cohen (Zone Books, 1991).
- Foucault, Michel, *Abnormal: Lectures at the Collège de France, 1974–1975*, tr Graham Burchell (Picador, 2003).
- Foucault, Michel, *Security, Territory, Population: Lectures at the Collège de France, 1977–1978*, tr Graham Burchell (Palgrave Macmillan, 2004).
- Hacking, Ian, *The Taming of Chance* (Cambridge University Press, 1990).
- Lévy, Bernard-Henri, *The Virus in the Age of Madness* (Yale University Press, 2020).

4

Recycling the Corpse

Introduction

In 2012 the International Consortium of Investigative Journalists (ICIJ) published a wide-ranging report on the global economy for cadaveric human tissue.[1] Over the course of an eight-month investigation across 11 countries, a transnational conglomerate of journalists tracked the procurement of so-called donated corpses in Ukraine to the development of medical implants, devices, and pharmaceuticals in Germany and to the distribution of biological products in the United States. In mapping the journey of the corpse and its fragmented parts from Eastern Europe to North America, the ICIJ revealed how a variety of commonly used medical treatments involve the recycling of cadaveric tissue. From cruciate ligament reconstructions to penis enlargements, heart valve replacements to orthopaedic surgery, and skin transplants, bone grafts, and bladder slings, the dead body materialises as a lucrative vessel in the twenty-first century for the repurposing of skin, blood, fat, muscle, and bone.

The origins of what the ICIJ describe as a 'shadowy market' in human body parts lie in the supply of anatomical cadavers to medical schools in the eighteenth and nineteenth centuries, which overwhelmingly involved trafficking Indigenous and African American remains throughout the British Empire.[2] The most notorious traders in this profitable enterprise were body snatchers and grave robbers – so-called resurrectionists and resurrection men – who until the enactment of the *Anatomy Act 1832* (UK) sought to obtain dead bodies by any means necessary. The Anatomy Act provided

---

1 The International Consortium of Investigative Journalists (ICIJ), *Skin & Bone: The Shadowy Trade in Human Body Parts* (Centre for Public Integrity, 2012).
2 For a history of trafficking the dead in Australia, England, and the United States in the eighteenth and nineteenth centuries see, Helen MacDonald, *Possessing the Dead: The Artful Science of Anatomy* (Melbourne University Press, 2010); Ruth Richardson, *Death, Dissection and the Destitute* (University of Chicago Press, 2001); Michael Sappol, *A Traffic of Dead Bodies: Anatomy and Embodied Social Identity in Nineteenth-Century America* (Princeton University Press, 2004).

DOI: 10.4324/9781003222163-4

for the first time a legal avenue for an executor of an estate or anyone in lawful possession of a corpse to supply it to a medical school for a modest fee. However, it was soon exploited by workhouses, prisons, hospitals, morgues, and funeral parlours to sell the unclaimed remains of paupers, prisoners, and Indigenous people for medical training and research.

Modern body snatchers, though they prefer to be called 'body brokers', still operate today to supply 'donated' corpses from tissue banks not only to medical schools but also profit-making companies, which then sell or lease the whole corpse or parts thereof to research institutes, pharmaceutical corporations, and medical training companies. Even though selling and buying organs and tissue for transplantation remains illegal in most countries around the world, body brokers have been able to generate profits by lawfully charging 'reasonable fees' for harvesting, transporting, packaging, and processing human remains. Since the 1980s, however, body brokers have diversified into different revenue streams by creating a global market for cadaveric tissue. Multinational conglomerates have sought waste products of different applications of work on the corpse in death-related trades – skin, blood, fat, muscle, and bone – for integration in biologically engineered medical products.[3] The allegations made by the ICIJ against RTI Surgical (formerly known as RTI Biologics) for its role in procuring cadaveric tissue and supplying it to for-profit companies for manufacturing a range of medical implants, devices, and pharmaceuticals suggests that body brokering is a profitable enterprise in the twenty-first century, and necrowaste has become a valuable commodity for sustaining human life.

This chapter investigates how the recycling of cadaveric tissue in the twenty-first century problematises the legal status of the corpse as either a person or a thing. Chapter 2 analysed how legal definitions of death are contingent upon economic rationality, while Chapter 3 contended that the laws of death registration recognise the value in counting the dead. In Chapter 4, I turn my attention to how legal doctrine on proprietary interests in the corpse has increasingly become challenged by technologies that repurpose cadaveric human tissue for a global market of biomedical products. I argue that the technologies involved in grinding down the corpse, transforming its parts into a paste, and integrating this substance in the generation of biomedical products dissect the dead body into *lucrative* waste and signal its use-value for human consumption.

---

3 These practices predominantly affect marginalised populations, especially those in the Global South who are already vulnerable to being trafficked in death. Kate Willson, et al., 'Human corpses harvested in multimillion-dollar trade', *Sydney Morning Herald*, 17 July 2012 <www.smh.com.au/politics/federal/human-corpses-harvested-in-multimilliondollar-trade-20120717-2278v.html>.

The starting point of this chapter is the question of the legal status of the corpse, which is unresolved in the common law. Since the seventeenth century, jurists have questioned whether the corpse constitutes in law a person or a thing. If it is held to be a thing, they have asked what obligations, if any, pertain to owning, trading, gifting, and exchanging human remains. On the other hand, if it is held to be a person, they have queried whether it is possible to endow the dead body with personhood, and if so, whether any rights or duties survive posthumously. The chapter contends that the persistence of the *res nullius* rule in the common law imagines a dead body that is *a priori* unique, whole, and bounded. It then turns to an examination of how the recycling of cadaveric tissue undermines this legal epistemology by transforming the human body and its parts into lucrative waste. Converting human remains into waste and repurposing it for biomedical products invites an alternative perspective of knowing the corpse by revealing the dead body to be intrinsically excessive. The chapter concludes by calling for a rethinking of how the corpse is defined in law, not in terms of whether it is a person or a thing, but rather through the discourse of lucrative necro-waste.

Res Nullius

The perennial question of the legal status of the corpse has long been unsettled in the common law. *Haynes' Case* was the first to define the corpse as neither a person nor a thing (*res nullius*) "but a lump of earth [that] hath no capacity".[4] William Haynes was caught disinterring graves, stealing the winding sheets found within, and reburying the dead bodies he exhumed. He was perhaps the first documented grave robber in the common law, or at least one of its most infamous protagonists, alongside the nineteenth-century body snatchers William Burke and William Hare. While it was indisputable that his nocturnal activities caused much offence to the sensibilities of Stuart society in the seventeenth century, the important legal issue in this case was whether Haynes could in fact steal the winding sheets from the dead or the living. The court held in this case that given dead bodies were not capable of owning anything, the winding sheets belonged to the executors of the estate, and thus Haynes could be convicted of the crime of theft. Even though the corpse was defined by the court as *res nullius*, or literally belonging to no-one, it was unequivocal, as William Blackstone remarked a hundred years later, that it was "not to be subject to the laws of property in the same manner as real earth".[5] In other words, *Haynes' Case* declared that the

4 *Haynes' Case* (1614) 77 ER 1389, 1389.
5 Margaret Davies and Ngaire Naffine, *Are Persons Property? Legal Debates About Property and Personality* (Ashgate, 2001) 107.

corpse was not a person who could own things, but neither was it a thing that could constitute property in itself.

Jurists have debated the amorphous contours of the *res nullius* doctrine in a handful of cases since the seventeenth century. In *Gilbert v Buzzard*, the ecclesiastical court rejected Mr Gilbert's petition to bury his wife in an iron instead of a wooden coffin to prevent her remains from being exhumed by the likes of William Haynes and his co-conspirators. The court justified its decision by defining the cemetery as a mere 'holding medium' and an iron coffin as an inappropriate vessel for burial, because it would impede the natural decomposition process.[6] If any right to possess a corpse was said to exist under the common law, it was not a proprietary right in perpetuity, but rather a limited right of possession constrained by the irreversible process of putrefaction. In *R v Stewart*, which concerned a dispute about who was responsible for paying for the burial of the deceased, the court reaffirmed *Gilbert* by emphasising that "[e]very person dying in this country . . . has *a right to Christian burial*".[7] What this meant, which was confirmed later in *Williams v Williams*, was that the executor of an estate has a non-proprietorial right of possession of a corpse until it is disposed of in the ground and once that corpse is buried, the right disappears.[8] While it was evident from *Gilbert*, *Stewart*, and *Williams* that the right to possess a corpse was not proprietary, but rather imposed a duty of custody upon the possessor until the body was buried, it was unclear from these cases how that duty fitted into existing categories of law.

The common law reinforced the doctrine that a corpse could not be subject to proprietary interests throughout the eighteenth and nineteenth centuries. The twentieth-century decision of *Doodeward v Spence*, however, articulated an exception to the 'no property' rule, whereby the labour or skill of the living transforms the corpse into something else. The High Court of Australia reasoned that the possession of an unburied human corpse was not necessarily unlawful – in fact it could be 'permanently possessed' – because medical schools and museums would simply cease to exist if they could not enforce proprietary rights in their anatomical displays and archaeological artefacts. While a corpse could never constitute a thing in itself, if

> a person has by the lawful exercise of work or skill so dealt with a human body or part of a human body in his lawful possession [such] that it has acquired some attributes differentiating it from a mere corpse awaiting burial, he acquires a right to retain possession of it, at least as against any person not entitled to have it delivered to him

6 *Gilbert v Buzzard* (1820) 161 ER 1342.
7 *R v Stewart* (1840) 113 ER 1007, 1009 (my emphasis).
8 *Williams v Williams* (1882) 20 Ch D 659.

for the purpose of burial, but subject, of course, to any positive law which forbids its retention under the particular circumstances.[9]

Recent case law in Australia has applied the *Doodeward* decision to justify that a spouse may possess human gametes extracted from their deceased partner either prior or after their death.[10] In *R v Kelly and Lindsay*, the English court relied upon the case when declaring that converting a corpse into a preserved specimen transformed it into a thing that could be owned.[11] This resulted in an adverse outcome for the defendants, who in imitating nineteenth-century body snatchers were convicted of stealing 35 human body parts from the Royal College of Surgeons. But the 'work or skill' doctrine in *Doodeward* sits unsteadily alongside the long-standing concept that only a contractual right to burial exists in common law, that is, an 'irrevocable licence' to remain undisturbed "at least until the natural process of dissolution" is complete.[12] It also remains incongruous with the jurisprudence of succession law, which since at least the twelfth century has developed rules by which the dead may exert proprietary rights over future generations.

The question of the legal status of the corpse has also been subject to much debate among philosophers, bioethicists, and legal scholars. Commentators have explored whether the corpse is a thing that can be lawfully owned, and theoretically traded, exchanged, or abandoned, and they have asked what obligations, if any, pertain to the bundle of proprietary rights in a dead body or parts thereof.[13] This approach builds upon

9 *Doodeward v Spence* (1908) 6 CLR 406, 414.

10 See, eg, *Bazley v Wesley Monash IVF Party Ltd* [2010] QSC 118; *Edwards; Re Estate of Edwards* [2011] NSWSC 478; *Re H, AE (No 2)* [2012] SASC 177.

11 *R v Kelly and Lindsay* [1998] 3 All ER 741. See also, *Yearworth v North Bristol NHS Trust* [2009] 3 WLR 118, which suggests that property law could apply to corpses, while the notion was rejected by US courts in *Calavito v New York Organ Donor Network* 486 F 3d 78 (2nd Cir 2006) and upheld in *Washington University v Catalona* 490 F 3d 667 (8th Cir 2007).

12 *Beard v Baulkham Hills Shire Council and Another* (1986) 7 NSWLR 273, 278. In *Smith v Tamworth City Council* [1997] NSWSC 197, Young J, quoting *Polhemus v Daly* 296 SW 442, 444 (1927), reiterated "while there is no right of private property in a dead body in the ordinary sense of the word, it is regarded as property so far as to entitle the next of kin to legal protection from unnecessary disturbance and violation or invasion of its place of burial".

13 See, eg, E Richard Gold, *Body Parts: Property Rights and the Ownership of Human Biological Materials* (Georgetown University Press, 1996); Rohan Hardcastle, *Law and the Human Body: Property Rights, Ownership, and Control* (Hart, 2009); Daniel Sperling, *Posthumous Interests: Legal and Ethical Perspectives* (Cambridge University Press, 2008). The idea of property as a bundle of relations between persons and things originates from Wesley Newcomb Hohfeld, *Fundamental Legal Conceptions of a Right as Applied in Judicial Reasoning* (Yale University Press, 1966).

the liberal argument that individuals should have exclusive control over the uses of their bodies. It is also grounded in the theory that legal exceptions to the 'no property' doctrine have gradually eroded the potency of the *res nullius* rule.[14] Yet the idea that the corpse could be subject to proprietary interests requires more than the preservation of body parts in a formaldehyde solution to transform it into something other than a 'mere corpse awaiting burial'. Rather, it demands that legal institutions determine the precise moment when the living person is metamorphosed into a dead thing, which is not without difficulty.[15] In Chapter 2, I discussed how inventions of medication, machinery, and surgical methods and treatments to prolong, sustain, and support life have problematised legal definitions of death. Whether it is due to technology that sustains the life of brain-dead persons or the biological functions of the human body that continue after the heart stops beating and the lungs cease breathing, I argued that the messy reality of death does not fit neatly into a legally distinct event.

The other side of this debate consists of scholars who dispute the notion that law can separate a person from its body or who denounce the objectification of the corpse and its derivatives.[16] Commentators who argue that the corpse cannot and should not be categorised in law as a thing have explored whether it is possible to endow it with legal personhood. While some advocates have looked to the modern law of testation to demonstrate how the dead exercise their legal personality over the living, others have asked whether the "death of the body is not the end of the biographical person".[17] The problem with conceiving of the corpse as a person, though, is that it relies upon a rationalist imagination of the dead body as *a priori* unique, whole, and bounded. The idea of posthumous personhood idealises the corpse as an undivided 'natural given' and either locates its personality in a disembodied will that transcends matter or assimilates it into the body itself, which ultimately

---

14 Muireann Quigley, 'Property in Human Biomaterials – Separating Persons and Things?' (2012) 32(4) *Oxford Journal of Legal Studies* 659, 661.

15 Roberto Esposito argues that the separability of persons, things and bodies is not possible: *Persons and Things: From the Body's Point of View*, tr Zakiya Hanafi (Cambridge University Press, 2015).

16 See, eg, Imogen Goold, Kate Greasley, Jonathan Herring and Loane Skene (eds), *Persons, Parts and Property: How Should We Regulate Human Tissue in the 21st Century* (Bloomsbury, 2016); Ngaire Naffine, 'When Does the Legal Person Die? Jeremy Bentham and the "Auto-icon"' (2000) 25 *Australian Journal of Legal Philosophy* 80; Loane Skene, 'Arguments Against People Legally 'Owning' Their Own Bodies, Body Parts and Tissue' (2002) 2 *Macquarie Law Journal* 165.

17 Sheila McGuiness and Margot Brazier, 'Respecting the Living Means Respecting the Dead Too' (2008) 28(2) *Oxford Journal of Legal Studies* 297, 303. See also, Richard Tur, 'The "Person" in Law' in Arthur Peacocke and Grant Gillett (eds), *Persons and Personality: A Contemporary Inquiry* (Basil Blackwell, 1987).

disintegrates through the decomposition process. Indeed, *Moore v Regents of the University of California* reveals the challenges of attributing personhood to a body that is inherently capable of fragmentation through the removal of tissue, blood, and cells during medical procedures.[18] This uncertainty has led scholars, such as Rosalind Atherton, to conclude that although the 'no property rule' is 'trite law', the corpse still retains a personality that must be held to be inalienable:

> [a]n acceptance of the 'thing-ness' of both corpses and body products for the purpose of fitting into a property law framework can be achieved – so long as the property idea does not overtake the essential 'person-ness' of the object in question.[19]

Doctrinal perspectives on whether the corpse is a person or a thing are not able to account for a global economy for cadaveric human tissue. The development of technologies for repurposing skin, blood, fat, muscle, and bone for biomedical products problematises legal epistemologies of the corpse. The reutilisation of waste from everyday procedures in death-related trades, whether that consists of post-mortem examinations or the disposal of human remains, divides the dead body into ever more parts that can be bought, sold, lent, or exchanged. The circulation of these practices around the world invites an alternative perspective of knowing the corpse by revealing the dead body to be intrinsically excessive. If the central question in the common law has been how to fit the corpse within the legal categories of person or thing, the remainder of the chapter explores instead whether the corpse can be rethought through a critical examination of the discourse of necro-waste.

Lucrative Waste

Funeral industries produce an abundance of waste. The corpse is disinfected, cleansed, shaved, stitched, bleached, and tinted. Arterial embalming involves pumping a formaldehyde solution through the body's arteries while draining its veins of blood and other fluids. Cavity embalming makes use of a 'trocar', which collects fluids, matter, gases, and bacteria from organs and injects chemical preservatives into

---

18 *Moore v Regents of the University of California* 51 Cal 3d 120 (1990). See further, Rebecca Skloot, *The Immortal Life of Henrietta Lacks* (Crown, 2010), which narrates how Henrietta Lacks, an African American woman, had her cervical cancer cells taken without her permission while undergoing treatment in the 1950s. The cells have been transformed by medical researchers into the HeLa cell line, which continues, despite criticism from Lacks' family, to be used today for research purposes.

19 Rosalind Atherton, 'Claims on the Deceased: The Corpse as Property' (2000) 8(1) *Journal of Law and Medicine* 361, 375.

the body's cavities. Cremation burns the body into bone grit, which is commonly referred to as ashes, but it also leaves behind heat-resistant medical implants, fine bone dust, and vaporised mercury. And alkaline hydrolysis, which consists of dissolving the corpse in a potassium hydroxide-water solution and heating the solution to 93 degrees Celsius for four hours, transforms the dead body into calcium phosphate and liquid effluence. Despite the differences between various modalities, and particularly the extent to which one may be more 'environmentally friendly' than another, technologies for the disposal of human remains create an array of debris.

The waste products of different applications of work on a corpse includes an ensemble of materials – fluids, gases, tissue, bone, skin, implants, chemicals, and effluence – discarded from post-mortem examinations, medical research and training, transplantation procedures, plastination techniques, and technologies for the disposal of human remains. This debris of the dead body, as highlighted by the ICIJ at the beginning of this chapter, is not always flushed into sewage drains or discarded in hazardous bins. It is increasingly sold and bought, lent and exchanged, and ultimately recycled in the generation of biomedical products for human consumption. While discussions of waste should not be confined to the funeral industry, it provides the most recognisable example of how a surplus of cadaveric tissue is produced, its use-value in the creation of biologicals, and consequently, how it transforms legal epistemologies of the corpse.

Philip Olson writes of the United States and Canadian funeral industry that its business model is structured around draining the corpse of "unwanted, useless, or obstructive matter" in the course of creating "a product of industrial art, an object to which new matter is added".[20] He provides the following example of how the funeral industry produces what he coins 'necro-waste' through embalming practices and technologies:

> During arterial injection, the embalmer drains blood from the corpse (typically by way of the incised jugular vein), while pumping diluted, pigmented embalming fluid (arterial fluid) into the body (usually through the carotid artery). The blood, along with some embalming fluid, flows down the embalming table and into a slop sink, which usually drains into either the municipal sewer system or a septic system.[21]

---

20 Philip R Olson, 'Knowing "Necro-Waste"' (2016) 30(3) *Social Epistemology: A Journal of Knowledge, Culture and Policy* 326, 331.

21 Ibid 331–332. For a history of how the funeral industry constructed knowledge of the human corpse in the nineteenth century see, John Troyer, 'Embalmed Vision' (2007) 12(1) *Mortality* 22.

The purpose of embalming is to arrest the visceral effects of death, to temporarily suspend the process of decomposition, and through the application of mechanical treatments and chemical substances present the corpse as if it was living, even if only for a couple of days prior to its disposal. Formaldehyde, methanol, phenol, putty, piping, and plastics are inserted into the corpse in a futile attempt to arrest the ravages of decay, which will, once the body is disposed of in the ground, contaminate the area around the gravesite. This means any liquids, gases, or solids deemed by the embalmer to be unnecessary to 'beautifying' the corpse (or could even hasten the decomposition process), such as blood, fat, tissue, organs, bone, or eyes, are removed and discarded as necro-waste. Funeral industries are highly regulated in different parts of the world; however, as Olson points out by way of example in North America, that does not mean that all aspects of its practices, such as the disposal of waste from the embalming table or what remains in the crematoria, are scrutinised by professional societies or state-based regulators. While human tissue, transplantation, or anatomy legislation in most countries prohibit the unauthorised selling and buying of tissue and organs, they are often reticent about waste disposal procedures.[22]

Technologies for the disposal of human remains fragment the corpse into *lucrative* necro-waste. The discourse of waste is commonly deployed to designate a thing no longer of value for human consumption. Yet as Myra J Hird explains, it is also "an inherently ambiguous linguistic signifier: anything and everything can become waste, and things can simultaneously be and not be waste".[23] Waste can signify a useless thing to be disposed of by one person, but for another that same thing may be regenerative of value. Indeed, "[f]or a long time cardiac valves and bones were considered to be surgical waste or *res nullius*, although this did not prevent their collection for surgical or therapeutic uses (replacement of cardiac valves, bone grafts)".[24] By adding the adjective 'lucrative' to the necro-waste generated by funeral industries when they prepare the corpse for disposal, I am denoting the profitability of the circulation of necro-waste in a global economy for cadaveric tissue. This

---

22   The *Human Tissue Act 2004* (UK) s 4 explicitly defines 'surplus tissue' as lawful waste, and in the United States, the case of *Albrecht v Treon*, 118 Ohio St 3d 348 (2008) declared that when a brain was removed during an autopsy, it was transformed into medical waste.

23   Myra J Hird, 'Knowing Waste: Towards an Inhuman Epistemology' (2012) 26(3–4) *Social Epistemology* 453, 454.

24   Sophie Chauveau, 'Human Tissues and Organs: Standardization and 'Commodification' of the Human Body' in Alexander von Schwerin, et al (eds), *Biologics, A History of Agents Made from Living Organisms in the Twentieth Century* (Taylor & Francis, 2013) 122.

is most apparent in the ICIJ's investigation on the trafficking of dead bodies from Eastern Europe to North America, which reveals the extent to which necro-waste can be resignified as valuable for the manufacture of medical devices, implants, and pharmaceuticals. The report shows how what was once designated as waste to be disposed of in drains can be recycled into a range of biomedical products:

> Cadaver bone – harvested from the dead and replaced with PVC piping for burial – is sculpted like pieces of hardwood into screws and anchors for dozens of orthopedic and dental applications. Or the bone is ground down and mixed with chemicals to form strong surgical glues that are advertised as being better than the artificial variety.[25]

The language of harvesting, extracting, and procuring cadaveric tissue recalls the discussion in Chapter 2 of how legal definitions of death are economised in the twenty-first century. While that chapter focused on how determinations of the moment of death have increasingly been conceptualised by law through the lens of economic analysis, it follows that technologies for the disposal of human remains have also become subject to the governing logic of economisation. Indeed, the ICIJ report demonstrates how cadaveric tissue is resignified through the lucrative discourse of necro-waste to facilitate its trafficking by vendors, circulation by brokers, and appropriation by pharmaceuticals. However, this economic concept does not only connote a theoretical framework for understanding how the fragmented corpse transforms into a commodity to be consumed, alienated, or abandoned.[26] The revaluation of the dead body as a producer of necro-waste disrupts legal epistemologies of the corpse as either a person or a thing. The idea of the corpse as infinitesimally divisible into ever smaller units of refuse reveals it to be intrinsically excessive. And repurposing necro-waste in biomedical products thus demands a different perspective of knowing the corpse.

Necro-Waste

In *The Accursed Share, Volume 1*, French philosopher Georges Bataille insists upon three luxuries of 'nature' that remove human beings from

---

25 ICIJ (n 1) 14.

26 See, eg, Lori Andrews and Dorothy Nelkin, *Body Bazaar: The Market for Human Tissue in the Biotechnology Age* (Crown Publishers, 2001); Michele Goodwin, *Black Markets: The Supply and Demand of Body Parts* (Cambridge University Press, 2006); Klaus Hoeyer, *Exchanging Human Bodily Material: Rethinking Bodies and Markets* (Springer, 2013); Lesley Sharp, *Bodies, Commodities, and Biotechnologies: Death, Mourning, and Scientific Desire in the Realm of Human Organ Transfer* (Columbia University Press, 2006).

the order of things: consumption, eroticism, and death. These luxuries do not return human beings to some kind of primordial personhood but instead to an impossible experience of animality. Animality is an ineffable or inaccessible experience because, according to Bataille, it has been lost through the development of humanity: the positing of an object, the use of tools, the enactment of laws, the advent of work, and the burial of the dead. It is difficult to define animality precisely because it exceeds meaning, especially in Bataille's writings, which often conflate it with the sacred amongst other concepts. The closest that Bataille ever comes to stabilising the meaning of animality is in the Theory of Religion where he states that "every animal is *in the world like water in water*".[27] This implies a liminal space between subjectivity and objectivity, immanence and transcendence, and knowledge and non-knowledge. In other words, it is a mythology of the end of times where humans become intimately inextricable from animals, where the living become indistinguishable from the dead and where persons are profoundly extracted from their singular existence in the world. The reason, then, why death is for Bataille "the simplest form of luxury" is that it theoretically returns human beings to the immediacy of a lost animality, where "there is generally no growth but only a luxurious squandering of energy in every form!"[28]

It is important to bear in mind that Bataille's reference to luxury in *The Accursed Share* is interchangeable with waste. The 'luxurious squandering' of death, for example, is wasteful, because it negates the singular existence of the human, it destroys what is most useful in them, and it wants nothing in return. Death annihilates the utility or value of someone, whether human or animal, and it reduces the body and its parts to waste. It also, as Bataille puts it, disrupts any attempts to render knowledgeable a lost animality as a useful thing amongst other things. On the other hand, death is productive of meaning; it is generative of new techniques of humanity, such as technologies of disposal, and to this extent it consumes the recycling of waste. What this indicates, then, is that death reveals the destruction of the use-value of the human body, and any attempt made to re-assimilate the lucrative waste of death into the order of things transforms an excess of meaning into the accumulation of knowledge.

Bataille's theory of waste represents death as the 'accursed share' in a restrictive economy of growth. He claims that by only focusing on production and accumulation, society has failed to understand the important role that waste and excess can assume in what he calls a general economy. Bataille explains that all systems in the world require energy

27 Georges Bataille, *Theory of Religion*, tr Robert Hurly (Zone Books, 1992) 19.
28 Georges Bataille, *The Accursed Share: An Essay on General Economy, Volume 1: Consumption*, tr Robert Hurley (Zone Books, 2007) 33.

to grow, and when they can no longer accumulate energy, or if the excess energy they have accumulated cannot be absorbed, "it must necessarily be lost without profit".[29] If energy is replaced by wealth and systems are replaced by human beings, it is easy to see how Bataille creates an economic theory that revolves around the play of growth and loss, accumulation and excess, and recycling and waste. He writes that if humanity ignores the important role that waste plays in the world economy in depleting 'surplus production', it will head inexorably towards death, the most 'catastrophic expenditure of excess energy':

> On the surface of the globe, for *living matter in general*, energy is always in excess; the question is always posed in terms of extravagance. The choice is limited to how the wealth is to be squandered. . .. The general movement of exudation (of waste) of living matter impels him, and he cannot stop it; moreover, being at the summit, his sovereignty in the living world identifies him with this movement; it destines him, in a privileged way, to that glorious operation, to useless consumption.[30]

By applying Bataille's theory of waste to legal epistemologies of the corpse, it is possible to comprehend why the problem of categorising the corpse as a person or a thing in law remains insurmountable. Necrowaste reveals an inevitable outpouring of excess; that is, it reveals the corpse as leaky, porous, and entangled with animal life. It is a surplus of tissue that transforms into something other than the corpse when dissected and exchanged. But it is also a surplus of knowledge of the corpse that haunts both its personhood and the 'thing-ness' of death. If the rationale of the legal cases discussed earlier is to recognise a human life behind the corpse or conceptualise the corpse as a thing that can be owned, necro-waste is a lucrative outcome of the instability of legal epistemology. Yet like the waste materials that are repurposed in recycling plants, to *know* necro-waste is to render it useful and valuable. When the dead body is dissected, fragmented, trafficked, and traded, it is recuperated in a global economy of cadaveric tissue that transforms knowledge of the corpse and resignifies necro-waste as valuable for human life.

In *Body Brokers: Inside America's Underground Trade in Human Remains*, the investigative journalist Annie Cheney documents her three-year exposé of the North American corpse trade. Preceding the ICIJ investigation by six years, Cheney highlights that nothing is wasted in the body brokering business. Whether bones are grounded into a fine paste for surgery or skin is "freeze-dried, stored, rehydrated, and

29 Ibid 21.
30 Ibid 23 (emphasis in original).

injected" directly into live patients, her book narrates a story of the recycling of cadaveric tissue.[31] The repurposing of necro-waste for medical devices, implants, treatments, and pharmaceuticals signifies in the words of Bataille a 'luxurious squandering' of death. The ICIJ investigation additionally shows an exponential growth in the circulation of cadaveric refuse and how its utilisation in the manufacture of biomedical products for living patients can be both beneficial and deleterious for their health. Bataille's theory of waste offers a philosophical base for rethinking the legal status of the corpse as a person or a thing. It refuses both categories by holding onto the corpse within a general economy of loss and growth, knowledge and non-knowledge, and waste and recycling. This theory requires a rethinking of how the human body is inherently capable of becoming waste, but also how that waste can be recycled into a valuable commodity for the sustenance of human life.

Catherine Waldby and Robert Mitchell use the concept of 'biovalue' to designate bodily waste that can be lucratively repurposed for medical research and training, and the generation of biomedical products. They are mainly concerned with tissue extracted from living bodies by hospitals that is "tacitly considered to have no value or significance for the patient", such as umbilical cord blood, cancerous tumours, fat deposits, and other medical waste.[32] In challenging the dualism of gift and commodity, biovalue waste is presented as 'surplus vitality' that "refers not to the stable and known properties of tissues but to the capacity of tissues to lead to new and unexpected forms of value".[33] The theory of necro-waste builds upon the idea of biovalue by speculating upon the limitless profitability of dissecting, fragmenting, circulating, and exchanging the corpse and its parts, but also, at the same time, recuperating each infinitesimal piece in an alternative perspective of knowing the corpse. As Olson writes,

[t]he human corpse can be conceptualized as a threat to public health, as a sacred object, as an object of considerable political or metaphysical power, as an aesthetic medium, as a source of nutrients, as a commodity, and as form of material waste – call it 'necro-waste'. Each of these ways of conceptualizing the corpse represents a different way of *knowing* the corpse, and no one body concept serves as the true and proper way of knowing the dead human body in all contexts or

---

31 Annie Cheney, *Body Brokers: Inside America's Underground Trade in Human Remains* (Broadway Books, 2006) 10.
32 Catherine Waldby and Robert Mitchell, *Tissue Economies: Blood, Organs, and Cells in Late Capitalism* (Duke University Press, 2006) 85.
33 Ibid 108.

for all purposes. Indeed, there are many ways of knowing the corpse because the corpse *means* many things.[34]

Conclusion

The question of whether the corpse and its parts can be categorised as a person or a thing in law, as both, or even nothing at all has not been resolved by jurists. It is unequivocal, on the one hand, that the 'no property' rule denotes that corpses should not be bought, sold or traded, seized by creditors to discharge a debt, or bequeathed in a will, and that if 'stolen' the responsible party cannot be prosecuted for the crime of theft, though they could of course be found guilty of gross indecency. Yet, on the other hand, the rule is suspended in numerous situations, not only those outlined in the cases discussed in this chapter but also exceptions permitted under legislation, such as the removal of body parts for organ and tissue transplantations, the extraction of human gametes for *in vitro* fertilisation and the disposal of 'medical waste' following a surgical procedure or post-mortem examination. While the legal status of the corpse may be ambiguous, what is certain is that law's epistemology is founded upon a search for the cadaver's facticity. The 'thing-ness' of the corpse, its matter, the apparent naturalness of its 'inanimate physicality', is contingent on locating an undivided and bounded body, or reifying the Cartesian dualism between matter and spirit. Even if the material existence of the corpse could be located prostrate in a grave, splayed on the dissection table, or plastinated in an anatomy museum, its "apparent unity", as Bruno Latour reminds us, "is only the superficial impression left by the routine of life".[35]

In *Brotherton v Cleveland*, the US Court of Appeals opined that

The recent explosion of research and information concerning biotechnology has created a marketplace in which human tissues are routinely sold to and by scientists, physicians and others. . .. As biotechnology continues to develop, so will the capacity to cultivate the resources in a dead body.[36]

The court attempted to imagine in this case the corpse as a useful commodity in a restrictive economy of growth. In this representation, the corpse is a mere thing that can be divided, lent, and sold once the living person evacuates its shell. The writings of Georges

---

34 Olson (n 20) 327 (emphasis in original).
35 Bruno Latour, 'Body, Cyborgs and the Politics of Incarnation' in Sean T Sweeney and Ian Hodder (eds), *The Body (The Darwin College Lectures)* (Cambridge, 2002) 127.
36 923 F 2d 477 (1991) at 481.

Bataille have been useful for explaining how this image of the corpse is ignorant of a general economy, that is, an excess of meaning that haunts the debris of death. His idea of the lucrative squandering of death is tantalising because it can show the way courts have conceived of the corpse based on rationalist constructions of an *a priori* unique, whole, and bounded body. However, where Bataille's theory of waste is most useful is in revealing how the dead body circulates in a general economy of play of growth and loss, accumulation and excess, and recycling and waste.

The chapter has travelled further than Bataille in calling for a rethinking of how the corpse is defined in law through the discourse of necrowaste. This is a waste-directed examination of the dead body and its parts that reveals how the human body can be designated as waste upon its death, transformed into a valuable commodity, and then manufactured into biomedical products for the sustenance of human life. Necrowaste challenges the legal doctrine of *res nullius*, as well as scholarly arguments that the corpse must be held as a unique, whole, and bounded person. This chapter asks the reader to take seriously the circulation of necro-waste in the world and not simply disregard it as wasteful knowledge. For to understand how human remains are converted into waste and repurposed for a profit – while comprehending the limits of law's capacity to know the corpse – it is possible to cultivate new legal epistemologies for intervening in a global economy for cadaveric human tissue.

Further Reading

- Bataille, Georges, *The Accursed Share: An Essay on General Economy, Volume 1: Consumption*, tr Robert Hurley (Zone Books, 2007).
- Cheney, Annie, *Body Brokers: Inside America's Underground Trade in Human Remains* (Broadway Books, 2006).
- Esposito, Roberto, *Persons and Things: From the Body's Point of View*, tr Zakiya Hanafi (Cambridge University Press, 2015).
- Goodwin, Michele, *Black Markets: The Supply and Demand of Body Parts* (Cambridge University Press, 2006).
- Olson, Philip R, 'Knowing "Necro-Waste"' (2016) 30(3) *Social Epistemology: A Journal of Knowledge, Culture and Policy* 326.
- Waldby, Catherine and Robert Mitchell, *Tissue Economies: Blood, Organs, and Cells in Late Capitalism* (Duke University Press, 2006).

Index

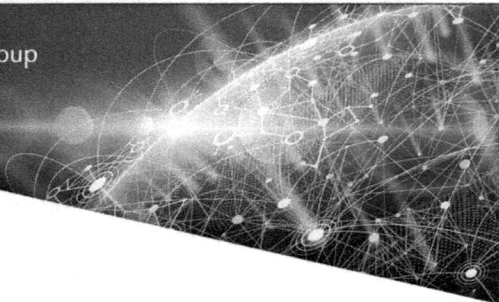

For Product Safety Concerns and Information please contact our EU
representative GPSR@taylorandfrancis.com
Taylor & Francis Verlag GmbH, Kaufingerstraße 24, 80331 München, Germany